ISLAM

ISLAM

Religion, History, and Civilization

Seyyed Hossein Nasr

HarperSanFrancisco
A Division of HarperCollins *Publishers*

Portions of this book were published in *Our Religions*, edited by Arvind Sharma and published by HarperSanFrancisco.

FIRST EDITION

Library of Congress Cataloging-in-Publication Data
Nasr, Seyyed Hossein.
Islam : religion, history, and civilization / Seyyed Hossein Nasr.
p. cm.
Includes bibliographical references and index.
ISBN 0-06-050714-4 (pbk.)
1. Islam—Essence, genius, nature. 2. Civilization, Islamic.
3. Islam—History. I. Title.
BP163.N2813 2002
297—dc21
2002032810

03 04 05 06 07 RRD (H) 10 9 8 7

FOR SINA

Contents

بسم الله الرحمن الرحيم

In the Name of God, the Infinitely Good, the All-Merciful

Introduction

Islam is both a religion and a civilization, a historical reality that spans over fourteen centuries of human history and a geographical presence in vast areas stretching over the Asian and African continents and even parts of Europe. It is also a spiritual and metahistorical reality that has transformed the inner and outer life of numerous human beings in very different temporal and spatial circumstances. Today over 1.2 billion people from different racial and cultural backgrounds are Muslim, and historically Islam has played a significant role in the development of certain aspects of other civilizations, especially Western civilization. Not only is Islam a major presence in today's world, but its influence is also evident in the history of the Christian West, not to mention that of India and other regions of Asia and Africa. That is why knowledge of Islam is so important for those concerned with the situation of contemporary humanity and those interested in Western intellectual and cultural history, as well as those attracted to the reality of religion and the world of the Spirit as such.

One would think, therefore, that the study of Islam would be widespread in the West and especially in America, which has a notable Muslim minority and which is now able to project so much power globally—including within the Islamic world. Such, however, is not the case, despite the rise of interest in Islam since the tragic events of September 11, 2001. Moreover, much that is presented today in the English language as the study of Islam by so-called experts is strongly colored by various prejudices and ideological biases, although there are exceptions. In fact, although Islamic studies have been carried out in the West for over a thousand years, in each period such studies have been distorted and tainted by a particular set of errors and deviations.

The study of Islam in the West began in the tenth and eleventh centuries. Because this was a time in which Europe was thoroughly Christian, Islam was seen as a Christian heresy, and its founder as an apostate. Soon the imminent threat to Western Christendom from Islam led many to call the Prophet of Islam the Antichrist, and the Quran itself was translated by order of Peter the Venerable in order to be refuted and rejected as sacred scripture. The Middle Ages were marked by strong religious opposition to Islam. Yet it was at this time that the West showed the greatest interest in Islamic thought, including philosophy and the sciences, and Islamic education, arts, and technology were greatly respected. The first translations into Latin of works of Islamic thought, ranging from philosophy and even theology to astronomy, mathematics, and medicine, belong to this period. Formal Islamic studies in the West may in fact be said to have begun during the Middle Ages.

The Renaissance perpetuated religious opposition to Islam, but also began to show disdain not only for Europe's own medieval past, but also for Islamic learning, although there were some exceptions. Furthermore, the emphasis on Eurocentrism during the Renaissance and the rise of humanism caused many European thinkers of that time to consider people of other civilizations and ethnic groups, including Muslims, inferior. Although Islamic studies were still carried on during the Renaissance, and in some places, such as Bologna, even within the framework of the older medieval respect for Islamic thought, in many places they were distorted by a sense of Western superiority and even hubris, characteristics that were to continue into the modern period.

The Enlightenment turned against the theological assertions of Christianity and substituted rationalism for a worldview based on faith. Moreover, it further developed the idea that there was only one civilization, the Western one, and that other civilizations were significant only to the extent of their contribution to Western civilization, which the French Encyclopedists referred to as *the* civilization *(la civilisation)*. Obviously in such a situation Islam and its civilization could only play an inferior and secondary role. Although some new translations of Islamic sources were made into European languages at this time and Islamic studies remained an intellectual and academic discipline, little was done to understand the teachings of Islam on their own terms. Many of the leading thinkers of this period, in fact, maintained the older European disdain for Islam, but at the same time tried to make use of some of its teachings to attack Christianity. Such a dual attitude toward Islam is evident in the works of Voltaire, among others.

During the nineteenth century, historicism in its absolutist sense took the center of the philosophical stage with Hegel, who considered all other civilizations stages in the march of the *Geist* in time leading to the final stage, which was supposedly realized in modern Western history. And yet this was also the period when the Romantic movement began, when many minds, tired of the rationalism of the Enlightenment, turned anew to the Middle Ages as well as to seeking meaning beyond the borders of the West. This was the period when many of the greatest spiritual masterpieces of Islamic literature, especially many of the Sufi classics, were translated into German, English, and French and seriously attracted major Western writers and thinkers, such as Goethe, Rückert, and Emerson. This was also the period when the exotic image of the Islamic East, with its mysterious *casbahs* and *ḥarams* full of nude females, developed, as reflected in nineteenth-century European art associated with "orientalism."

Moreover, this period marked the beginning of official oriental studies, including Islamic studies, in various Western universities, often supported by colonial governments such as those of Britain, France, the Netherlands, and Russia. Oriental studies, in fact, developed as an instrument for furthering the policy of colonial powers, whether they were carried out in Central Asia for use by the Russian colonial office or in India for the British government. But there were among the orientalists in the late nineteenth and first half of the twentieth century also a number of noble scholars who studied Islam both objectively and with sympathy, such as Thomas Arnold, Sir Hamilton Gibb, Louis Massignon, and Henry Corbin. Later Western orientalists who belong to this tradition include Marshall Hodgson, Annemarie Schimmel, and several other important scholars. But the main product of the orientalist manner of studying Islam remained heavily biased not only as a result of the interests of those powers it was serving, but also through the absolutization of current Western concepts and methodologies that were applied to Islam with the sense of superiority and hubris going back to the Renaissance definition of the "European man."

The last half of the twentieth century witnessed a major transformation in Islamic studies in the West, at least in certain circles. First of all, a number of acutely intelligent and spiritually aware Westerners who realized the spiritual poverty of modernism began to seek wisdom in other worlds. Some turned to the objective and unbiased study of the deepest teachings of Islam, which only confirmed for them the reality of the presence of a perennial *sophia* at the heart of all heavenly inspired religions. This group, which includes René Guénon, Frithjof Schuon, Titus Burckhardt, Martin Lings, Gai Eaton, Michel Vâlsan, William Chittick, Michel Chodkiewicz, James Morris, Vincent Cornell, and many other notable contemporary Western writers on Islam, has produced a wholly new type of literature in the West as far as Islam is concerned. It has created a body of writings rooted in the authentic teachings of Islam, yet formulated in the intellectual language of the West and based on the confirmation—not the denial—of the spiritual teachings on which traditional Western civilization itself was founded.

Furthermore, during this same period authentic representatives of the Islamic tradition, those who were born and brought up in that tradition, began to study Western thought and languages and gradually to produce works in European languages on Islam that were not simply apologetic (as had been the earlier works in English of a number of Indian Muslim writers), but explained clearly and without compromise the teachings of Islam in a manner comprehensible to Westerners. Needless to say, during this period there also appeared a large number of completely modernized Muslim writers who wrote about Islam not from within the Islamic worldview, but from the point of view of the ever changing categories of modern and, more recently, postmodern Western thought.

Finally, a younger generation of scholars have appeared on the scene during the past few years who are both Muslim and Western. Either they are Muslims born in the West or Westerners who have openly embraced Islam, have lived in the Islamic world, and know it well from within. Scholars belonging to this category are now beginning to occupy a number of academic positions in Europe and America and to produce pertinent works of an authentic nature on various aspects of Islamic studies.

Despite the presence of such groups, however, the anti-Islamic approach to Islamic studies continues in many circles.

Some academics continue to apply non-Islamic, and in fact purely secularist, concepts drawn from various currents of Western philosophy and social sciences to Islam. And then there are the political ideologues, who often have little knowledge of Islam yet are presented as experts on the subject; from them one hears the most egregious anti-Islamic statements touted in the media and in popular books as authentic knowledge of Islam. They are joined in this chorus by a number of Christian voices from extremist groups who speak as if they were living in twelfth-century France at the time of the Crusades, but who are at the same time completely devoid of knowledge of traditional Christian theology, not to mention Christian humility and charity.

Each period of the study of Islam in the West has produced its own literature usually colored by the prejudices of the period, which have been for the most part anti-Islamic. There is, in fact, no religion in the world about which Western authors have written so much and at the same time in such a pejorative way as Islam. And yet, despite the persistence of this genre of writing and in fact its increase since the tragedies of September 11, 2001, authentic works on Islam based on truth and the intention to create mutual understanding rather than hatred, works of the sort that were practically nonexistent in the earlier part of the twentieth century, are now readily available in the English language. The present book seeks to serve as an introduction to Islam and its civilization in the spirit of such works, that is, in the spirit of mutual understanding and respect between Islam and the West and on the basis of the truth of the teachings of Islam as it has been understood by its adherents over the ages.

Islam is not only a religion; it is also the creator and living spirit of a major world civilization with a long history stretching over fourteen centuries. Islamic history concerns the historic existence of the peoples of many lands, from North Africa to Malaysia, over vast spans of time. It has witnessed the creation of some of the greatest empires and the integration into a single social order of many diverse ethnic and linguistic groups. Islamic history has, moreover, directly affected the history of Europe for over a millennium and has been in turn deeply affected by the West since the advent of the colonial period. Islamic history has, furthermore, been profoundly intertwined with the history of India since the seventh century and with certain aspects of Chinese history for the past millennium (and to some extent even before that, going back to the century following the rise of Islam).

Islam created a civilization that has covered the middle belt of the Old World for over a millennium. This civilization produced great intellectual figures, a distinct art and architecture, dazzling achievements in science and technology, and an equitable social order based on the teachings of the Quran. Its thinkers, poets, musicians, and artists created works that deeply influenced Western as well as Indian and even to some extent Chinese art and thought. Its scientists formulated theories and carried out practices that were widely emulated by Western scientists during the Middle Ages and even the Renaissance.

In this book I deal briefly with both Islamic history and the intellectual dimensions of Islam and its civilization, but in such an introductory work it is not possible to also adequately cover the arts and sciences. Yet it must be remembered how significant they are for an understanding of Islamic civilization and various Islamic cultures. Because Islam, like Judaism, does not permit the making of a Divine image, it has produced an aniconic sacred art in which the presence of God is indicated by geometric patterns, arabesques, rhythmic repetitions, and empty space pointing to unity rather than by icons. Islam has made the chanting and writing of the Word of God, that is, the Quran, its highest sacred arts. Hence, the central role of Quranic psalmody and calligraphy, which are ubiquitous in Islamic civilization. Next it has honored architecture, which creates spaces in which the Word of God reverberates and therefore, like calligraphy, is related in its essential form and function to the Divine Word. Furthermore, Islamic art has paid special attention to the arts that concern us most in our everyday lives, such as the art of the dress, the carpet, and various daily utensils. As for painting, although some consider the Persian miniature, from which the rich Mogul and Turkish schools of miniature derive, one of the greatest schools of painting in the world, painting has always been closely related to the art of the book and has never occupied the same central role in Islamic civilization that it has done in the West.

Wherever Islam went, it did not destroy the local culture, but transformed it into an Islamic reality. What were rejected were elements of a clearly un-Islamic nature. As a result,

Islamic civilization developed into several distinct cultural zones including the Arabic, Persian, Black African, Turkic, Indian, Malay, and Chinese. In each of these zones Islamic culture and art were to have a certain distinct local style while preserving their universal Islamic character. For example, Moroccan and Turkish architecture are both distinct, yet deeply Islamic in character. Also in calligraphy certain local styles such as the *maghribī* in Morocco, Andalusia, and Algeria and *shikastah* in Persia developed, while in the same lands one sees the *kūfic*, *thuluth*, and *naskhī* styles, which are universal throughout the Islamic world.

Islamic civilization produced a very rich tradition in the aural arts of poetry and music. There are very few civilizations of the past two millennia in which so much attention has been paid to poetry and in which poetry has occupied such an exalted position as in Islam. All major Islamic languages, such as Arabic, Persian, Turkish, Swahili, Bengali, and Urdu, as well as more local languages, such as Sindhi, Pushtu, and Hausa, have a very rich poetic tradition, and poetry plays a far greater role in private and public life in the Islamic world today than it does in the contemporary English-speaking world. Sufi poetry in Persian has been called by some the most sublime and diversified mystical poetry in the world, and Jalāl al-Dīn Rūmī, one of the greatest of the Persian Sufi poets, who is also deeply venerated by the Turks, is in fact the most widely read poet in America today.

Apart from military music, which through Ottoman channels became the origin of the European and later American military bands, and other forms of music associated with certain vocations or occasions such as weddings, Islamic civilization discouraged an exteriorizing music that would simply intensify the worldly passions within the soul. Rather, it drew music toward the inner dimension of human existence. In the hands of the Sufis, music became a steed with which the soul could journey from the outward rim of existence to the inner courtyard of the soul, where the Divine Presence resides. Islamic civilization created many musical instruments, such as the *tār* and the *'ūd*, which were to find their counterparts in the guitar and the lute in the West. Furthermore, Islamic philosophers and theoreticians of music wrote notable works on theory, structure, notation, and the effects of music on the soul as well as the body, works that are attracting new interest in the West today, where much attention is being paid again to the philosophy of music and especially the relation between music and physical and psychological healing.

The contributions of Islamic science are so great and complex that they cannot even be summarized in a proper and meaningful way in a short introduction. Suffice it to say, for some seven centuries (the eighth through the fourteenth and fifteenth century), Islamic science was, from the point of view of creativity, at the forefront of science considered globally. Not only did Muslims synthesize Greco-Alexandrian, ancient Mesopotamian, Iranian, Indian, and to some extent Chinese science, but they created many new sciences or added new chapters to the ancient sciences. For example, in mathematics they expanded the study of the geometry of the Greeks and created the new disciplines of trigonometry and algebra. Likewise, in medicine they furthered the studies of Hippocratic and Galenic medicine while diagnosing and distinguishing new diseases, discovering new remedies, and proposing new theories. The same can be said for numerous other sciences, from alchemy to astronomy, from physics to geology. The global history of science has as one of its central chapters Islamic science, without which there would have been no Western science. And yet Islamic science had an understanding of nature and the role of the sciences of nature in the total scheme of knowledge that was very different from what developed in the West with the seventeenth-century Scientific Revolution.

In trying to understand Islamic civilization, it is essential to remember not only the diversity of the arts and the sciences, but also the diversity of theological and philosophical interpretations of Islamic doctrines and even of Islamic Law. There is nothing more erroneous than thinking that Islam is a monolithic reality and that Islamic civilization did not allow the creation or subsistence of diversity. Although a sense of unity has at all times dominated everything Islamic, there has always existed a diversity of interpretations of the religion itself as well as various aspects of Islamic thought and culture. The Prophet of Islam even considered the diversity of views of the scholars of the Islamic community a blessing from God. When one studies Islamic civilization, one sees not only differences of language and dress, writing and singing, color of skin and physical features, cuisine, and response to different climatic conditions, but also different interpretations of verses of the

Quran, sayings of the Prophet, and tenets of the Divine Law as well as theological and philosophical questions. And yet a remarkable unity predominates in the civilization, as it does in the religion that created that civilization and has guided its history over the ages.

In this book I hope to provide a clear and succinct introduction to the religion of Islam as well as its history and civilization, at least in its intellectual aspects. The present work, as all of my earlier writings on Islam, is written from within the Islamic perspective and from the traditional point of view, from the perspective of the sacred and universal teachings of Islam as they were revealed and later transmitted over the ages. This point of view stands opposed to both modernism and its complement, so-called fundamentalism, and speaks from the view of those Muslims who have remained faithful to their sacred traditions despite the onslaught of the secularizing forces that have invaded the Islamic world during the past two centuries and reactions to those forces in the form of narrow "fundamentalism" or extremism of one kind or another.

The norm in the Islamic world even today, despite all the political tragedies that have befallen it, is not what many in the media and popular literature in the West claim. It is not religious extremism or "fundamentalism"; nor is it secularist modernism. The norm is traditional Islam, in comparison to which both secularist modernism and "fundamentalism" are extremes. At the present juncture of human history, it is of the utmost importance for Westerners who seek understanding and goodwill to comprehend clearly the norm with respect to which all forms of extremism must be measured. And it is important to distinguish authentic knowledge of the subject matter at hand from ideologically distorted accounts of it.

The present book is related especially to two other of my works: *Ideals and Realities of Islam* and *The Heart of Islam.* The first was written over thirty-five years ago and deals solely with classical Islam from the traditional point of view. According to some it has become a "classic" introduction to this subject in many languages and has been reprinted numerous times over the years. It does not, however, deal with Islamic history and the intellectual aspects of Islamic civilization, as does the present book. *The Heart of Islam,* which is being published nearly at the same time as this book, deals with various aspects of Islam in direct response to the challenges posed by the tragedy of September 11, 2001, and the questions raised in the minds of many Westerners as a result of that horrific event. Each of these works is distinct unto itself, and yet this book in a sense complements the other two. What they have in common, besides the subject matter of Islam, is the universalist perspective and respect for other religions, to which the Quran refers so often and which has been my perspective in all of my writings for more than four decades.

I hope that this short work will facilitate better mutual understanding between Westerners and Muslims, an understanding essential to the survival of both East and West. I wish to thank Stephen Hanselman of Harper San Francisco for making the appearance of this volume possible. This work was originally a part of *Our Religions*, edited by A. Sharma and published by Harper. It has been revised and includes a new introduction and bibliography. I also wish to thank Katherine O'Brien for preparing the manuscript of this work for publication.

Wa mā tawfīqī illā bi'Llāh
Bethesda, Maryland
June 2002
Rabīʿ al-awwal A.H.1423

1

Islam and the Islamic World

The Significance of the Study of Islam Today

These days, the reality of Islam penetrates the consciousness of contemporary Westerners from nearly every direction. Whether it is consequences of the decades-old Middle Eastern conflict between Arabs and Jews, the aftershocks of the upheavals of the Iranian Revolution, the civil war in Yugoslavia, where Muslim Bosnians were caught between feuding Orthodox Serbs and Catholic Croats, the breakup of the Soviet Union and the sudden appearance of a number of Muslim republics, the tragic events of September 11, 2001, in New York and Washington and their aftermath, or the ever more frequent use of Muslim names in the pages of American newspapers, it seems that the name and reality of Islam have come to constitute an important dimension of the life of humanity today, even in America and Europe. And yet there is no major religion whose study is more distorted in the West than Islam, which is too familiar to be considered an exotic religion and yet distinct enough from Christianity to pose as the "other," as it has in fact done in the West for well over a millennium.

The study of Islam as a religion and as the "presiding Idea," or dominating principle, of a major world civilization is of great significance for the West not only because it makes better known the worldview of more than a billion two hundred million people ranging from blue-eyed Slavs and Berbers to Black Africans, from Arabs to Malays, and from Turks and Persians to Chinese. It is also significant because Islam and its civilization have played a far greater role than is usually admitted in the genesis and development of European (and American) civilization. Today Islam constitutes the second largest religious community in Europe and has a population almost the size of Judaism's in America. But most of all, the study of Islam is significant because it concerns a message from God revealed within that very Abrahamic world from which Judaism and Christianity originated. The Islamic revelation is the third and final revelation of the Abrahamic monotheistic cycle and constitutes a major branch of the tree of monotheism. It is, therefore, a religion without whose study the knowledge of the whole religious family to which Jews and Christians belong would be incomplete.

Islam as the Final Revelation and Return to the Primordial Religion

Islam considers itself the last major world religion in the current history of humanity and believes that there will be no other plenary revelation after it until the end of human history and the coming of the eschatological events described so eloquently in the final chapters of the Quran, which is the verbatim Word of God in Islam. That is why the Prophet of Islam is called the "Seal of Prophets" *(khātam al-anbiyā')*. Islam sees itself as the final link in a long chain of prophecy that goes back to Adam, who was not only the father of humanity *(abu'l-bashar)*, but also the first prophet. There is, in fact, but a single religion, that of Divine Unity *(al-tawḥīd)*, which has constituted the heart of all messages from Heaven and which Islam has come to assert in its final form.

The Islamic message is, therefore, none other than the acceptance of God as the One *(al-Aḥad)* and submission to Him *(taslīm)*, which results in peace *(salām)*, hence the name of Islam, which means simply "surrender to the Will of the One God," called Allah in Arabic. To become a Muslim, it is sufficient to bear testimony before two Muslim witnesses that "There is no god but God" *(Lā ilāha illa'Llāh)* and that "Muḥammad[1] is the Messenger of God" *(Muḥammadun rasūl Allāh)*. These two testimonies *(shahādahs)* contain the alpha and omega of the Islamic message. One asserts the unity of the Divine Principle and the other the reception of the message of unity through the person whom God chose as His final prophet. The Quran continuously emphasizes the doctrine of Unity and the Oneness of God, and it can be said that the very raison d'être of Islam is to assert in a final and categorical manner the Oneness of God and the nothingness of all before the Majesty of that One. As the chapter on Unity *(sūrat al-tawḥīd)* in the Quran asserts: "Say He God is One; God the eternally Besought of all. He begetteth not nor is He begotten. And there is none like unto Him" (112:1–4).[2]

The term "Allah" used in this and other verses of the Quran refers not to a tribal or ethnic god, but to the supreme Divine Principle in the Arabic language. Arab Christians and Arabized Jews in fact refer to God as Allah, as do Muslims. The Arabic word "Allah" is therefore translatable as "God," provided this term is understood to include the Godhead and is not identified solely with Christian trinitarian doctrines. Islam, in asserting over and over again the Omniscience and Omnipotence as well as Mercy and Generosity of God as the One, puts the seal of finality upon what it considers to be the universal religious message as such. It also places the primordial reality of human beings directly before the Divine Presence, and it is this primordial nature hidden at the heart of all men and women that the Quran addresses. That is why, according to the Quran, even before the creation of the world, God asked human beings: "Am I not your Lord?" and not one person, but the whole of humanity, both male and female, answered: "Yes, verily we bear witness" (7:172). As the final religion of humanity, Islam is the last divinely orchestrated response of yes to the pre-eternal Divine question, the response that constitutes the very definition of being human.

By virtue of its insistence upon Divine Oneness and pre-eternal response of humanity to the lordship of the One, Islam also signifies the return to the primordial religion and names itself accordingly (*dīn al-fiṭrah,* the religion that is in the nature of things, or *dīn al-ḥanīf,* the primordial religion of

Unity). Islam is not based on a particular historical event or an ethnic collectivity, but on a universal and primordial truth, which has therefore always been and will always be. It sees itself as a return to the truth that stands above and beyond all historical contingencies. The Quran, in fact, refers to Abraham, who lived long before the historic manifestation of Islam, as *muslim* as well as *ḥanīf*; that is, belonging to that primordial monotheism that survived among a few, despite the fall of the majority of men and women of later Arab society, preceding the rise of Islam, into a crass form of idolatry and polytheism that Muslims identify with the age of ignorance *(al-jāhiliyyah)*. Islam is a return not only to the religion of Abraham, but even to that of Adam, restoring primordial monotheism without identifying it with a single people, as is seen in the case of Judaism, or a single event of human history, as one observes in the prevalent historical view of the incarnation in Christian theology.

The Prophet asserted that he brought nothing new but simply reaffirmed the truth that always was. This primordial character of the Islamic message is reflected not only in its essentiality, universality, and simplicity, but also in its inclusive attitude toward the religions and forms of wisdom that preceded it. Islam has always claimed the earlier prophets of the Abrahamic world and even the pre-Abrahamic world (e.g., Noah and Adam) as its own, to the extent that these central spiritual and religious figures play a more important role in everyday Islamic piety than they do in Christian religious life. Also as a result, Islam has been able to preserve something of the ambience of the Abrahamic world in what survives of traditional Islamic life; Westerners who journey to traditional Muslim areas even today are usually reminded of the world of Hebrew prophets and of Christ himself.

It was not, however, only the Abrahamic world that became included in Islam's understanding of itself as both the final and the primordial religion. As Islam encountered non-Semitic religions later on in Persia, India, and elsewhere, the same principle of the universality of revelation applied. The result was that many of the philosophies and schools of thought of the ancient world were fairly easily integrated into the Islamic intellectual perspective, as long as they conformed to or affirmed the principle of Unity. In this case they were usually considered remnants of the teachings of earlier prophets, constituting part of that vast family that brought the message of God's Oneness to every people and race, as the Quran asserts. One of the results of this primordial character of Islam, therefore, was the formation and development of the Islamic intellectual tradition as the repository for much of the wisdom of the ancient world, ranging from the Greco-Alexandrian heritage to that of India.

As every veritable omega is also an alpha, Islam as the terminal religion of humanity is also a return to the primordial religion. In its categorical and final formulation of the doctrine of Unity, it returns to the primordial message that bound Adam to God and that defines religion as such. The universality of Islam may be said to issue from this return to the primordial religion, whereas its particularity may be said to be related to its finality, which has provided the distinctive form for one of the world's major religions.

Unity and Diversity Within the Islamic Tradition: Sunnism and Shī'ism

Unity cannot manifest itself without entering into the world of multiplicity, yet this manifestation is the means whereby humanity is led from multiplicity to Unity. Islam's great emphasis on Unity, therefore, could not prevent diversity on the formal level, nor could Islam have integrated a vast segment of humanity with diverse ethnic, linguistic, and cultural backgrounds without making possible diverse interpretations of its teachings. These teachings, nevertheless, lead to that Unity residing at the heart of the Islamic message as long as the interpreters of them remain within the framework of Islamic orthopraxy and orthodoxy considered in their widest and most universal sense. The Islamic religion, therefore, is comprised of diverse schools and interpretations that are deeply rooted and united in the principles of the Islamic revelation.

The most important elements among those that unite the vast spectrum of schools composing Islam in its orthodox manifestations, this term being understood in a metaphysical as well as a theological and juridical manner, are the two testimonies *(shahādahs)* themselves. By virtue of the first *shahādah*, that is, "There is no god but God," all Muslims confirm the unity of the Divine Principle and the reliance of all things on Him. Through the second *shahādah*, "Muḥammad is the messenger of God," they accept the prophethood of the Prophet and thereby become specifically Muslims. Moreover, all Muslims agree that the Quran is the verbatim revelation of God. They also agree about its text and content; that is, no variant texts are found among any of the schools, although the exegetical meaning can, of course, differ from one school to another. Muslims also agree concerning the reality of the afterlife, although again there are various types and levels of interpretation of the teachings of the Quran and the *Ḥadīth* (sayings of the Prophet) concerning eschatological (end-time) matters. Muslims are also united in the main rituals performed, ranging from the daily prayers to fasting to making the pilgrimage, although here again there are certain small differences in ritual details among the various schools of Islamic Law.

Finally, one must mention the spirit emanating from the Quranic revelation and the grace *(barakah)* of the Prophet, issuing from his being and his *Sunnah* (deeds) and resulting from the very fact that Islam is a living religion with its channels to Heaven open here and now, not only an event of past history. These less definable factors are nevertheless powerful elements that unify Islam and the Islamic world. They also possess more concrete manifestations, especially in Sufism, Islam's mystical or esoteric dimension, which in the form of Sufi orders covers the whole of the Islamic world and provides a hidden yet powerful force for the unity of that world. The presence of these factors is ubiquitous and can hardly be denied even externally. Their effect is to be seen all the way from the manner in which Quranic chanting in Arabic transforms the soul of Muslims everywhere, whether they are Arabs or Bengalis, to the architecture and urban planning of Islamic cities, whether they are in Morocco or Persia, from the way in which traditional Muslim men dress to the way people take off their shoes when entering a traditional Muslim house, whether it is in Senegal or Malaysia.

Within this unity, which is perceptible even to outsiders, diversity exists on various levels—exegetical, legal, theological, philosophical, social, and political. In fact, the Prophet has said, "The difference of view among the scholars *('ulamā')* of my community is a blessing from God." Throughout the history of Islam there have existed diverse interpretations of the Quran and *Ḥadīth*, different schools of law, many theological and philosophical interpretations, and political claims on the basis of the interpretation of religious texts. These differences have sometimes led to not only fierce religious rivalries, but also wars, a phenomenon that is, however, not unique to Islam. Differences, however, have never been able to destroy the unity of Islam as either a religion or a civilization. It was in reference to the danger of excessive theological and religious dispute that the Prophet said that the Islamic community would divide after him into seventy-two schools, of which only one would be completely in the right and would possess the complete truth. In this saying he predicted not only the contention of the various schools that would appear in time, but also the persistence of the truth, which could not in its most universal sense be other than that of the two *shahādahs*. Furthermore, the Prophet was not referring to the vertical and hierarchical dimensions of Islam and levels of interpretation of its truths, which do not represent diversity and opposition in the same sense and to which we shall turn later in this work.

Nearly all Muslims belong to one of three groups: Sunnis, Shīʿites, and Khārijites. This last group comprises those who opposed the claim of both ʿAlī and Muʿāwiyah to the caliphate, which will be discussed later. Khārijites have always been few in number and today their inheritors, known as ʿIbādīs, remain confined to Oman and southern Algeria. The most important division within Islam is between Sunnism and Shīʿism. The vast majority of Muslims, that is, about 86 to 87 percent, are Sunnis, a term that comes from *ahl al-sunnah wa'l-jamāʿah*, "followers of the *sunnah* of the Prophet and the majority." About 13 to 14 percent of Muslims are Shīʿites, a word that derives from *shīʿat ʿAlī*, "the partisans of ʿAlī (ʿAlī ibn Abī Ṭālib)." They in turn are divided into Twelve-Imām Shīʿites, Ismāʿīlīs, and Zaydīs. The Twelve-Imām, or Ithnā ʿashariyyah, Shīʿites are by far the most numerous, comprising some 150 million people living mostly in present-day Iran, Iraq, Lebanon, the Persian Gulf States, eastern Saudi Arabia, Afghanistan, Azerbaijan, Pakistan, and India. Iran, Iraq, Azerbaijan, and Bahrain have majority Twelve-Imām Shīʿite populations, while in Lebanon the Shīʿites constitute the largest single religious community.

The Ismāʿīlīs played an important role in Islamic history and established their own caliphate in Egypt during the Fāṭimid period in the fourth/tenth and fifth/eleventh centuries.[3] Today, however, they are scattered in various communities, mostly in a number of towns of Pakistan and India, but also with important concentrations in East Africa, Syria, and the Pamir and Hindu Kush regions of Afghanistan, Pakistan, and Tajikistan. They also have a notable community in Canada, consisting mainly of emigrants from East Africa, India, and Pakistan. Ismāʿīlīs are divided into two main branches, one with its center in India and the other in scattered communities under the direction of the Aga Khan, whose followers consider him their imām (or spiritual and temporal leader). It is difficult to give an exact figure for the members of this community, but altogether the Ismāʿīlīs are estimated to be a few million in number. Finally, several million Zaydīs, who among various schools of Shīʿism are theologically the closest to Sunnism, reside almost totally in Yemen.

The Shīʿites separated from the Sunnis upon the death of the Prophet when the question of succession became vital. The majority of the community chose Abū Bakr, the venerable friend of the Prophet, as the first caliph (from the Arabic *khalīfah*, meaning, in this context, the vicegerent of the Prophet of God), while a small number believed that ʿAlī, the cousin and son-in-law of the Prophet, should have become caliph. The problem was, however, more profound than one of personalities. It also concerned the function of the person who was to succeed the Prophet. The Sunnis believed that the function of such a person should be to protect the Divine Law, act as judge, and rule over the community, preserving public order and the borders of the Islamic world. The Shīʿites believed that such a person should also be able to interpret the Quran and the Law and in fact possess inward knowledge. Therefore, he had to be chosen by God and the Prophet, not by the community. Such a figure was called *Imām.*[4] Although such a person did not share in the Prophet's prophetic function *(nubuwwah),* he did receive the inner spiritual power of the Prophet *(walāyah/wilāyah).* Moreover, the Shīʿites identified this person with ʿAlī ibn Abī Ṭālib, whom they believed the Prophet chose as his successor before his death. Shīʿism is, therefore, very much related to the family of the Prophet *(ahl al-bayt),* the later Imāms all being descendants of ʿAlī and Fāṭimah, the daughter of the Prophet.

The Shīʿite Imām is also considered by Shīʿism as the only legitimate ruler of the Islamic community, hence the rejection by Shīʿites of the first three caliphs as well as the later Sunni caliphates. Twelve-Imām Shīʿites therefore have rejected (until the Iranian Revolution of 1979), all existing political authority ever since the short-lived caliphate of ʿAlī came to an abrupt end with his assassination. They believe that the twelfth Imām, the Mahdī, is in occultation *(ghaybah),* that is, not outwardly present in this world and yet alive. All legitimate political power must derive from him, and he will appear one day to bring justice and peace to the world as part of eschatological events that will bring human history to a close. Since 1979 and the Iranian Revolution—as a result of which Shīʿite religious figures rule directly in Iran—new interpretations of the relation between religious and governmental authority have been made, but the significance and role of the hidden Imām remains unchanged.

Shīʿism became particularly consolidated with the martyrdom of the third Imām, Ḥusayn ibn ʿAlī, who was killed in the first/seventh century along with most of the members of his, and therefore the Prophet's, immediate family by the army of the Umayyad caliph Yazīd in Karbalā' in Iraq. His body is buried there, but his head was brought to Cairo, where it was interred and a shrine was built for it, a shrine that remains the heart of that city to this day. Henceforth, Twelve-Imām Shīʿism continued as a protest movement of increasing political significance, but did not gain complete political power over any extensive area of the Islamic world until the Ṣafavids conquered Persia in 907/1501 and established Twelve-Imām Shīʿism as the official state religion. As for Ismāʿīlism, it had major political manifestations earlier in Islamic history, especially with the establishment of the Fāṭimids, who ruled a vast area from Tunisia to Syria, with their base in Egypt, from 297/909 to 567/1171. Turning to Zaydism, its power base became Yemen, where its followers ruled until the invasion by Egypt in 1962.

Shīʿism, however, must not be considered simply a political movement. Rather, Shīʿism developed its own schools of law, theology, philosophy, and other religious sciences, including methods of Quranic exegesis. Debates and sometimes confrontations continued in the various religious sciences between Shīʿite and Sunni positions, dialogues that played no small role in the development of religious thought in both worlds. However, despite periods of Sunni-Shīʿite political, and sometimes military, confrontation and the exploitation of these differences by Western powers that began to colonize the Islamic world in the eleventh/seventeenth century, Sunnis and Shīʿites have also lived in peace in many climes and times. Especially during the past century, their religious scholars have sought to create accord on the basis of the many elements that unite them within the embrace of the totality of the Islamic tradition.

Besides Sunnism and Shīʿism, other diversities of a less significant nature need to be mentioned. For example, there are theological and philosophical differences among various schools mentioned in the class of writings with the title *al-milal wa'l-niḥal,* literally "religious groups and schools of thought." Many of these can be compared to, let us say, the Bonaventurian and Thomistic interpretations of medieval Christian theology, but others developed into what one can call a veritable sect in contrast to Sunnism and Shīʿism, which constitute Islamic orthodoxy and should not be referred to as sects. Sects within the Islamic world, all of which are small, include some, like the ʿAlawīs of Turkey and Nuṣayrīs of Syria, who remain in some way related to the Islamic religion. Others, like the Druze of Lebanon and adjacent areas, or the Bahā'īs, originally of Persia but now spread throughout many lands, broke away from Islam and became independent religious communities, although they are, nevertheless, related historically to Islam. In any case these small sects and groups constitute a part of the tapestry of certain parts of the Islamic world and contribute to the diversity to be found within

Islamic society, although their nature and teachings are in most cases very different from each other and from those of the vast Islamic majority.

The Islamic Community and Ethnic and Cultural Groups Within It

One of the key concepts in Islam is that of the *ummah,* or the totality of the people who are Muslims and constitute the Islamic world. Islam sees history itself in religious terms and refers to other people not primarily by their linguistic or ethnic affiliations but by their religious identity, hence the reference to the *ummah* of Moses or Jesus found so often in Islamic texts when discussing Judaism or Christianity. The Islamic *ummah* is one, bound by solidarity to the Quranic message of Divine Oneness and Sovereignty, the messengership of the Prophet, and acceptance of the Divine Law *(al-Sharīʿah)*. Muslims are united by the powerful bond of brotherhood and sisterhood, a bond that is felt strongly to this day despite all the turmoil that has pitted and continues to pit Muslims against one another. God has warned against such divisiveness in the verse: "And hold fast, all of you together, to the cable of God and do not separate" (3:103). One cannot understand Islam without gaining a sense of the significance of the concept of *ummah* and the reality of that community which, although no longer politically united, is nevertheless a single religious community characterized by that sense of brotherhood *(ukhuwwah)* so much emphasized by the Quran and the Prophet.

The *ummah* is not, however, composed of a single ethnic, racial, or cultural group. Islam was, from the beginning, a religion that addressed the whole of humanity and strongly opposed all forms of racism and tribalism, as the following famous Quranic verse points out so clearly: "O mankind! Lo! We have created you male and female, and have made you nations and tribes that ye may know one another! Lo! the noblest of you, in the sight of God, is the most righteous" (49:13). The later history of Islam was to bear out its global destiny. Over the centuries Arabs and Persians, Turks and Indians, Black Africans and Malays, Chinese and even some Tibetans, Mongolians, and Slavs have become part of the *ummah*, and during the past few decades Islam has been spreading in Europe, North and South America, and, to some extent, Australia. There is hardly any ethnic or racial group in the world that does not have some members belonging to the Islamic *ummah*. This can be seen physically in the annual pilgrimage to Mecca, where people from every corner of the globe assemble to worship at the house rebuilt by Abraham in honor of God who is One after the original temple, built according to Islamic belief by Adam himself, had fallen into ruin.

The Spread and Demographic Growth of Islam

Islam began in Arabia, where the revelation was first received by the Prophet, but then spread rapidly among the Persians and Black Africans, and soon thereafter among Turks,

Chinese, Indians, and many other ethnic groups. The spread of Islam occurred in waves. In less than a century after the establishment of the first Islamic society in Medina by the Prophet, Arab armies had conquered a land stretching from the Indus River to France and brought with them Islam, which, contrary to popular Western conceptions, was not, however, forced on the people by the sword. In some places, such as Persia, it took several centuries for the majority of people to embrace Islam, long after Arab military power had ceased. Later, Islam spread peacefully through Sufi teachers among the Turkic people of Central Asia, before their migration south to the western regions of Central Asia, and finally westward through northern Persia to Anatolia. It also spread peacefully, again mostly by means of Sufism, through most of the Indian Subcontinent from the fifth/eleventh century onward and throughout Java, Sumatra, and Malaya from the eighth/fourteenth century on. Since about the twelfth/eighteenth century, Islam has been also spreading, yet again mostly through the agency of Sufism, ever farther into the African continent south of the Sahara, moving both southward and inland. During the Ottoman occupation of the Balkans, Islamic communities were established, especially in Albania, Macedonia, Bosnia, and Kosovo; some of these communities are over five hundred years old. It is generally believed that Islam is the fastest-growing religion in the world today.

These phases of the spread of Islam brought peoples of many different ethnic and cultural backgrounds into the single *ummah*. Yet, like the types of diversity already mentioned, this ethnic diversity has not destroyed the unity of the *ummah* at all, but rather has enriched it, for unity is not uniformity. In fact, it stands diametrically opposed to uniformity. When one looks at the Islamic world today, one sees several major ethnic and cultural zones with their own subdivisions but unified in their attachment to the Islamic tradition and composing in their totality the Islamic *ummah*.

The Global Distribution of Muslims and Zones of Islamic Civilization

Most people in the West automatically identify Muslims with Arabs. Today, however, Arabs compose about a fifth of the world Muslim population. But they remain of central importance in the *ummah* because of their historical role in the Islamic world; their language, which is that of the Quran; and the significance for all Muslims of the sacred sites of Islam that lie within the Arab world, especially the cities of Mecca and Medina, in the Hejaz in present-day Saudi Arabia, and old Jerusalem, which was historically in Palestine but has been occupied by Israel since 1967. Today over 220 million Muslim Arabs live from Mauritania to Iraq. The Arab identification is made not ethnically but linguistically; that is, a person whose mother tongue is Arabic is considered an Arab. The vast majority of Arabs are, of course, Muslims, although in certain Arab countries, such as Lebanon, Egypt, Jordan, and Syria, as well as among the Palestinians, there is a sizable Arab Christian population; and before the partition of Palestine, highly culturally Arabized Jewish communities also existed in most Arab countries. There are many subcultures within the Arab world, but the main division is between the eastern and the western Arabs, the line of demarcation being somewhere in Libya. Each part, while profoundly Islamic and Arabic, has its local cultural color and traits, which can be seen in the literature, architecture, and other arts and cuisine of the two areas.

The second oldest ethnic and cultural zone of the Islamic world is the Persian, comprising not only the people of present-day Iran but also those of similar ethnic and linguistic stock including the Kurds and the people of Afghanistan (including the Pushtus), Tajikistan, and parts of Uzbekistan and Pakistan. Together they number over 100 million people and are of particular historic and cultural importance because it was the Persians who, along with the Arabs, built classical Islamic civilization, and Persia has always been one of the most important artistic and intellectual centers of the Islamic world. Furthermore, the Persian language is, after Arabic, the most important language of Islamic civilization and the only other classical language in Islamic civilization spoken and written beyond the land of its native speakers. For more than a millennium it was the primary literary medium used by people from Iraq to China and, outside of Persia proper, especially in India.

Closely related ethnically to the various Iranian groups and the world of Persian culture and, like the Persians, of Indo-European stock are the Muslims of the Indian Subcontinent.

They constitute the largest single group of the followers of Islam, consisting of over 400 million people in Pakistan and Bangladesh, which are predominantly Muslim, as well as in India, Sri Lanka, and Nepal, where they are in a minority. India, in fact, has well over 130 million Muslims, the largest single minority in the world. The most prominent language of Muslims of this area is Urdu, related closely to both Sanskrit and Persian, although many other Indian languages, such as Punjabi, Sindhi, Gujarati, and Tamil, are also used by Muslims. Bengali must be considered, along with Urdu, as the other major literary Islamic language of the Subcontinent.

After the Arabs and Persians, the next important group, in terms of its participation in Islamic civilization and its role in Islamic history, is the Turkic people, who are spread from the Balkans to eastern Siberia. The Turks have played a major role in the political life of Islam during the past millennium. It was the Turks who created the powerful Ottoman Empire, stretching from Algeria to Bosnia, an empire that lasted for about seven centuries, until World War I. But the Turkic people are not limited to the Turks of the Ottoman world and present-day Turkey. Several of the now independent republics of Caucasia and Central Asia are ethnically and linguistically Turkic, although some are culturally very close to the Persian world. There are also people of Turkic stock within Russia itself. There are perhaps more than 150 million people belonging to this ethnic group, with languages that are neither Semitic, like Arabic, nor Indo-Iranian, like Persian, but Altaic. They represent a distinct zone within Islamic civilization that has been in constant interaction with the Arabic and Persian worlds over the centuries.

Islam spread over areas of Black Africa very early in its career, and Black African Muslims have played an important role in Islamic history; the caller to prayer *(mu'adhdhin)* of the Prophet, Bilāl, was himself a black. Black African Muslims had established thriving empires in sub-Saharan Africa by the seventh/thirteenth century, and Islam in Africa has been and continues to be a vital and vibrant force, even during the period of European colonization. Today over 150 million Black African Muslims, as distinct from the Arab and Berber North Africans, compose a notable zone of Islamic civilization. Black Africans speak many different languages, such as Fulani, Hausa, and Swahili, and constitute many subcultures. But the main division in this part of the Islamic world is between East and West Africa, although, again, a strong bond of unity exists between the two areas. They are bridged by numerous links, including the Sufi orders, which have had a major role in the spread of Islam in Africa and are still very active in most regions of Muslim Black Africa.

Islam spread into the Malay world later than in the areas already mentioned, starting in the eighth/fourteenth century. Today this world includes the most populated and ethnically homogeneous of all Islamic countries, Indonesia. It has a rich Islamic culture embracing, in addition to Indonesia, Malaysia, Brunei, the southern Philippines, and certain areas of Thailand and Kampuchia as well as a part of Singapore. This zone is characterized by its use of Malay as its main literary tongue and the adaptation of Islam to a particular natural and cultural environment very different from what one finds in the cradle of classical Islamic civilization in the Middle East. More than 220 million Muslims are scattered in this vast area, which includes thousands of islands as well as the Malay Peninsula.

Less is known about Chinese Muslims than any other group in the Islamic world. Their number is estimated anywhere from 25 to 100 million, and they are scattered all over China, with the main concentration being in the western province of Sinkiang (the old Eastern Turkestan). They are an old community—there are records of Muslims in Canton in the first/seventh century—and they have created a distinct Chinese Islamic culture of their own, including their own distinct style of Arabic calligraphy. There is also a corpus of Chinese Islamic literature, most of which remains unknown to the outside world. But Muslims remain an important minority in China, as they do in certain other countries from Burma in South Asia to Sweden in northern Europe.

Mention must also be made of the parts of the *ummah* living in Europe and America, although their number is relatively small. Over 20 million Muslims live in various European countries. Some, including the Bosnians, who are of Slavic stock, and the Albanians, of Albania, Macedonia, and Kosovo, belong to communities that are centuries old, as are small communities of Turkish and even Bulgar origin. The rest are predominantly immigrants who have come to Europe since World War II and consist mostly of North Africans in

France; Indians, Pakistanis, and Bangladeshis in Great Britain; and Turks and Kurds in Germany. There are also a number of European converts to Islam. Muslims now constitute important communities in many areas and have even posed cultural and social challenges in some countries, such as France.

There is no doubt that many of the slaves brought over from Africa to North America were originally Muslims, but their religion was gradually forgotten. Since the 1930s, however, Islam has been spreading among African Americans and now represents a notable religious voice in America. Today, about 6 million Muslims live in North America, consisting not only of African Americans and Arabs, but also some Persians, Turks, and people of the Indian Subcontinent who have migrated to America during the past century and especially during the past few decades. A number of Americans and Canadians of European stock have also embraced Islam. Thus, the Islamic community continues to grow in North America as well as in Central and South America, where, in Brazil, Argentina, Trinidad, and several other areas, there exist sizable Muslim populations.

The Islamic *ummah* therefore comprises many ethnic, linguistic, and cultural elements: Semites, Indo-Iranians, Turks, Black Africans, Malays, Chinese, and others speaking numerous languages—especially Arabic, which is a Semitic tongue, but also Iranian, Indo-European, Altaic, and African languages. Although concentrated in Asia and Africa, the members of the *ummah* are also scattered over the other four continents and constitute important minorities in many lands and nations. They possess their own languages and cultures and yet participate in the greater whole that is the *ummah* and the Islamic civilization of which they are all members. Islam is like a vast tapestry into which all these local cultural modes and varieties are woven like arabesques; the larger pattern they make reflects the Oneness of the Divine Principle.

2

Islam as Religion

The Islamic Understanding of the Role of Religion in Human Life

The term in Arabic that corresponds most closely to "religion" is *al-dīn*. Whereas "religion" comes from the Latin root *religare*, meaning "to bind" and therefore by implication that which binds us to God, *al-dīn* is said by some Arabic grammarians and Quranic commentators to derive from *al-dayn*, which means "debt." *Al-dīn*, therefore, means the repaying of our debt to God and involves the whole of our life, because we are indebted to God not only for individual gifts, but most of all for the gift of existence itself. For the Muslim mind, it is the most obvious of facts and greatest of certitudes that by ourselves we are nothing and God is everything, that we own nothing by ourselves and that all belongs to God according to the Quranic verse: "God is the rich *(ghaniy)* and ye are the poor *(fuqarā')*" (47:38). We are poor in our very essence; we are poor not necessarily in an economic, social, or even physical sense, but in an ontological one. Therefore, all that we are and all that we have belongs to God, for which we are indebted to Him and for whose gifts we must give thanks *(shukr).* Religion, or *al-dīn,* which is inseparable from the sense of the reality of this "debt," therefore, embraces the whole of life and is inseparable from life itself.

In the Islamic perspective, religion is not seen as a part of life or a special kind of activity like art, thought, commerce, social discourse, or politics. Rather, it is the matrix and worldview within which these and all other human activities, efforts, creations, and thoughts take place or should take place. It is the very sap of the tree of life as well as the total environment in which this tree grows. As has been said so often, Islam is not only a religion, in the modern sense of the term as it has been redefined in a secularized world in which the religious life occupies at best a small part of the daily activities of most people. Rather, Islam is religion as a total way of life. Islam does not even accept the validity of a domain outside the realm of religion and the sacred and refuses to accord any reality to the dichotomy between the sacred and the profane or secular, or the spiritual and the temporal. Such terms as "secular" and "profane" in their current understanding cannot even be translated exactly into the Islamic languages in their classical form, and current terms used to render them in these languages are recently coined words usually derived from the idea of worldliness, which is not the same as "secular" or "profane." The Quran often refers to this-worldliness, which is contrasted with the abiding realities of the other world (*al-dunyā* and *al-ākhirah*), but this dichotomy must not be confused with the division between the sacred and the secular or profane. One can be worldly in a completely religious universe in which worldliness itself has a religious meaning, but one cannot be secular in such a universe unless one claims the independence for a particular realm of life from religion and the sacred. Islam asserts that there is no extraterritoriality in religion and that nothing can exist legitimately outside the realm of tradition in the sense of religion and the application of its principles over the space and temporal history of a particular human collectivity. Moreover, Islam claims this all-encompassing quality not only for itself, but also for religion as such.

Religion, then, must embrace the whole of life. Every human thought and action must be ultimately related to the Divine Principle, which is the source of all that is. Both the existence of the cosmic order, including the human world, and all the qualities to be found in the cosmos come from God and are therefore inseparable from His Nature and Will and the theophanies of His various Names and Qualities. Religion is there to remind forgetful human beings of this metaphysical reality and, on the more practical level, to provide concrete guidance so that men and women can live according to the Will of God and at the highest level gain, or rather regain, the knowledge of His Oneness and the manner in which all multiplicity is ultimately related to the One. Every act that individuals perform, every thought they nurture in their minds, and every object they make must be related to God, if they are to remain faithful to the true nature of things and of themselves. Religion is the reality that makes the realization of this nexus between the human world in all of its aspects and God possible. Therefore, its role in human life is central. It can even be said, from the Islamic point of view, that religion in its most universal and essential sense is life itself.

The Private Aspects of Religion

Although Islam has this all-embracing concept of religion, it does divide the injunctions and teachings of religion into what concerns private life and what is related to the public domain, although these two aspects are not seen as totally separate. On the contrary, their interrelatedness is constantly emphasized. The private aspects deal primarily with all that concerns the inner rapport of men and women with God. They involve prayer in all its modes, from individual supplication *(al-du'ā)*, to the canonical prayers *(al-ṣalāh)*, to the invocation of the Names of God *(al-dhikr)*, which is quintessential prayer, practiced especially by the Sufis and identified at the highest level with the prayer of the heart. The other major rites, such as fasting and pilgrimage, all of which will be treated later, also pertain to the private aspects of life. Yet these rites also have a strong public aspect, as do the canonical prayers, which are often performed in community with other Muslims. Of course, the canonical prayers can always be performed alone and in private—except for the congregational prayers of Friday, which naturally involve the public, whether small or large in number.

Islam also provides the principles for human actions as they pertain to private life. First, a human being's treatment of his or her own body is governed by the Divine Law *(al-Sharī'ah)*. This includes not only hygienic and dietary regulations of religious importance, but also the religious duty to take care of the body, religious injunctions concerning all sexual practices, and religious prohibition of harming the body, including, of course, suicide, which is forbidden by Islamic Law and considered a great sin. Many of these elements are, needless to say, found in other religions, a fact to which Islam points as support for the view that religion is inseparable from the normal life of humanity.

Islam, like Judaism, considers dietary regulations to be of religious significance and a means of sacralizing everyday life. Muslims are forbidden *(ḥarām)* to drink alcoholic beverages, eat pork and all its derivatives, or consume certain other types of meat, such as those of carnivorous animals. Meat from animals whose consumption is permitted *(ḥalāl)* must be sacrificed in the Name of God. There is therefore the full awareness of the religious conditions that alone permit the slaughtering of animals. This sacrificial view has, needless to say, the deepest effect on the relation between human beings and the animal world.

Other private aspects of life, such as one's relation with one's parents, spouse, children, other relatives, friends, and neighbors, are also governed by religious teachings. All of these domains are regulated by both legal and moral injunctions of a religious character. For example, the Quran exhorts children to be kind and to respect their parents. This is a moral injunction based on religious authority. Laws also exist concerning the distribution of a person's inheritance among various members of the family. This is a legal injunction, again, based on religious authority. Altogether, as far as the private sector of life is concerned, the teachings of Islam emphasize men and women's duties toward their own bodies and souls in relation to God as well as close bonds within the family, with the result that the family constitutes the central institution in Islamic society and family bonds have always been and remain to this day very strong in the Islamic community.

It is important to emphasize here that the attitude, so prevalent in the modern world, that a person's body and life are his or her own to do with as he or she pleases is totally alien to Islam. Our bodies and lives are not our own; they are God's. We did not create either our bodies or our lives. They belong to God, and we must treat them with this truth in mind, with a sense of duty and responsibility in light of God's injunctions as revealed in the Quran and explained by the Prophet. There is no such thing as human rights without human responsibilities. All human rights derive from the fulfillment of responsibilities to the Giver of human life.

The most private aspect of life is of course the inner, spiritual life, in which men and women approach God to a greater or lesser extent according to the degree of their spiritual capacity and inwardness; one of the Names of God mentioned in the Quran is the Inward *(al-Bāṭin)*. The Islamic revelation contains elaborate teachings pertaining to this most inner, private aspect of human life, teachings that have been formulated and elaborated over the centuries by Islamic masters of the path toward inwardness, the vast majority of whom have been Sufis. But even this most inward dimension of religion has its public and outward complement, as God Himself is not only the Inward, but also the Outward *(al-Ẓāhir)* according to the Quranic verse: "He is the First *(al-Awwal)* and the Last *(al-Ākhir)* and the Outward *(al-Ẓāhir)* and the Inward *(al-Bāṭin)* and He knows infinitely all things" (57:3).

The Public Aspects of Religion

As a religion that emphasizes equilibrium and justice in all aspects of human life, Islam also accentuates the outward and public aspects of religion to complement the inward and private ones. According to Islam, religion is not only a matter of private conscience, although it certainly includes this dimension; it is also concerned with the public domain, with the social, economic, and even political lives of human beings. There is no division between the Kingdom of God and the kingdom of Caesar in the Islamic perspective. Rather, all belongs to God and must therefore be regulated by Divine

Law and moral injunctions that come from Him and are religious in nature.

The public aspects of Islam concern every part of the community qua community, stretching from the local social unit all the way to the *ummah* itself and even the whole of humanity and creation. There are no relations between human beings and between them and the rest of creation that do not possess a religious significance, starting with the relations between members of the most concrete community, the family, neighborhood, village, or tribe, and leading to greater and less palpable units such as a province or state (in the traditional Islamic sense of the term), to *dār al-islām*, or the "Abode of Islam," and Muslim minorities in non-Islamic lands, to the whole of humanity and finally to creation itself. Islamic injunctions therefore embrace non-Muslims, whose treatment is covered by Islamic Law. Human relations considered by Islam include social transactions and interactions ranging from duties and responsibilities to one's neighbors and friends to those toward orphans and the destitute, stranger Muslims, and non-Muslims. Some of the teachings of Islam in this domain are general moral instructions, such as being charitable or just in all situations and toward all people and also other creatures of God. Others are formulated in concrete laws that have governed Islamic social behavior over the centuries, including the personal laws concerning such matters as marriage, divorce, and inheritance, which belong to the private as well the public domain.

One important public aspect of Islam concerns economic activity. In contrast to Christianity, which, in its early history, displayed a certain disdain for mercantile activity and in which there are no explicit economic injunctions as far as its revealed sources in the New Testament are concerned, the Quran and the *Ḥadīth* contain explicit economic teachings. These teachings form the foundation of what has come to be known more recently as Islamic economics, although it might be mentioned here that the economic views of St. Thomas Aquinas resemble Islamic teachings in many ways. There are Islamic injunctions relating to how transactions should be carried out, the hoarding of wealth as well as its distribution, religious taxation, endowment *(awqāf)*, economic treatment of the poor, the prohibition of usury, and many other injunctions that became formalized over the centuries in various Islamic institutions and laws.

The bazaar has always played an important religious role in Islamic society and continues to do so to this day. The guilds that have been responsible for the making of objects, from rugs to pottery, and the carrying out of projects of public economic significance, from the digging of underground waterways *(qanāt)* to the construction of roads and buildings, have always had a direct religious aspect and have been usually associated with the Sufi orders. According to the Islamic perspective, there is no such thing as economics considered in and of itself. What is called economics today has always been considered in Islam in relation to ethics, and religious injunctions have been promulgated to check and limit human greed, selfishness, and avarice, in an effort to prevent them from completely destroying the exercise of justice that is so strongly emphasized in Islam.

The public aspects of religion in Islam are also concerned with military and political life, which is not to say that every Muslim ruler or military leader has followed the Islamic injunctions fully. There is an elaborate code of conduct in war based primarily on the defense of *dār al-islām* rather than aggression, fair treatment of the enemy including prisoners of war, prohibition of killing innocent civilians, and the like. There is much talk today about *jihād*, usually translated "holy war." Actually it means "exertion" in the path of God, and in its outward aspect it is meant to be defensive and not aggressive. Whatever misuse is made of this term by extremists in the Islamic world or Western commentators of the Islamic scene does not change the meaning of outward *jihād* in the traditional Islamic context as an exertion to preserve one's religion or homeland from attack in the traditional Islamic context. As for inward *jihād*, it means to battle the negative tendencies within the soul, tendencies that prevent us from living a life of sanctity and reaching the perfection God has meant for us.

Islam is said to be the first civilization to have developed a fully codified international law that takes such matters as war and peace between nations into consideration. Likewise, there are extensive Islamic teachings concerning political rule, although, in contrast to the case of the social and economic activities, the Quran and *Ḥadīth* are less explicit about the actual form that government should take and much more explicit about the general nature of good government and just rulers. It was only later in Islamic history that the classical theories of Islamic government were developed, a subject to which we shall turn later.

What Does Islam Teach Us About Religion?

Islam teaches that religion is in the nature of human beings. To be human is to be concerned with religion; to stand erect, as men and women do, is to seek transcendence. Human beings have received the imprint of God on the very substance of their souls and cannot evade religion any more than they can avoid breathing. Individuals here and there may reject religion or a society may turn against its God-given religion for a short time, but even those events possess a religious significance. Men and women are created in the "form" *(ṣūrah)* of God, according to the famous Prophetic *Ḥadīth*. Here *ṣūrah* means the reflection of God's Names and Qualities, for otherwise God is formless and imageless. Also, God breathed into human beings His Spirit according to the verse: "I have made him and have breathed into him My Spirit" (15:29). To be human is to carry this Spirit at the depth of one's being and therefore to be concerned with religion and the author of all religion, who has breathed His Spirit into us.

According to Islam, as in all traditional teachings, men and women did not ascend from lower forms of life, but descended from on high, from a Divine prototype. Therefore, humanity has always been humanity and has always had religion. The first man, Adam, was also the first prophet. Religion did not evolve gradually during the history of humanity, but has always been there, in different forms but always containing the eternal message of Divine Oneness until, as a result of forgetfulness, its teachings were neglected and corrupted, only to be renewed by a new message from Heaven. Monotheism did not evolve from polytheism. Rather, polytheism is a decadent form of monotheism necessitating the ever newer revelations that have characterized human history.

It is religion alone that can bestow meaning on human life, because it and it alone issues directly and in an objective manner from the same Divine Source as human life itself. Religion alone can actualize the potentialities within human beings and enable them to be fully themselves. It is only with the help of Heaven that we can become what we are eternally in the Divine Presence. Religion provides that supreme knowledge which is the highest goal of the intelligence and reveals the nature of that Reality which is also supreme love and the ultimate goal of the will. Religion is the source of all ethics and values, providing the objective criteria for the worth of human actions and deeds. It is also the source of veritable knowledge of both the Divine Principle and the created order in its relation to that Principle as well as the bearer of those principles that constitute the science of beauty and of forms in a traditional civilization.

Islam cannot accept a human world in which religion is irrelevant. It can understand perfectly what it means to rebel against God and His prophets and has a fully developed doctrine concerning the nature of evil, the trials and tribulations of the life of faith, the dangers of unbelief, and the consequences of being responsible, as a being endowed with freedom to choose, before God. But the idea of humanity without religion as normal and a world in which the being or nonbeing of God is irrelevant and inconsequential as acceptable are totally rejected by Islam, which sees religion as the sine qua non of human life. Indeed, it is a human being's relation to the Absolute, whatever that relation might be, that determines his or her relation to the relative. The loss of religion for the individual can only mean separation from both inner beatitude and the beatitude of the Beyond and, for a society as a whole, a sure sign of the disintegration of that society as a viable human collectivity.

The Foundations of Islam

THE QURAN: ITS SIGNIFICANCE AND STRUCTURE

The Quran is the central theophany of Islam, the verbatim Word of God revealed to the Prophet by the archangel Gabriel and transmitted by him in turn to his companions, who both memorized and recorded it. It was later assembled in its present order under the instruction of the Prophet and written down in several manuscripts. During the caliphate of 'Uthmān a few years after the death of the Prophet, the definitive text was copied in several examples and sent to the four corners of the newly established Islamic world. There exists only one version of the text of the Quran, one that is agreed on by all schools of Islam, a text considered to be sacred in its entirety, not only in meaning but also in form.

The name of the sacred scripture of Islam by which it has become famous, especially in the West, is the Quran, or Koran, from the Arabic *al-Qur'ān*, which means "The Recitation." But the sacred text has many other names, each referring to an aspect of it. It is also known as *al-Furqān*, "The Discernment," for it contains the principles for both intellectual and moral discernment. Another of its well-known names is *Umm al-kitāb*, "The Mother Book," for it is the ultimate source of all knowledge and the prototype of the "book" as container of knowledge. It is also known as *al-Hudā*, "The Guide," for it is the supreme guide for people's journey through life. In traditional Islamic languages, it is usually referred to as the Noble Quran *(al-Qur'ān al-majīd* or *al-karīm)* and is treated with the utmost respect as a sacred reality that surrounds and defines the life of Muslims from the cradle to the grave. The verses of the Quran are the very first sounds heard by the newborn child and the last the dying person hears on his or her way to the encounter with God.

In a sense, the soul of the Muslim is woven of verses and expressions drawn from the Quran. Such expressions as *inshā' Allāh*, "If God wills," *al-ḥamdu li'Llāh*, "Thanks be to God," and *bismi'Llāh*, "In the Name of God," all used by Arab as well as non-Arab Muslims alike, punctuate the whole of life and determine the texture of the soul of the Muslim. Every legitimate action begins with a *bismi'Llāh* and ends with an *al-ḥamdu li'Llāh*, while the attitude toward the future is always conditioned by the awareness of *inshā' Allāh*, for all depends on the Divine Will. These and many other formulas drawn from the Quran determine the attitude toward the past, the present, and the future and cover the whole of life. The daily prayers that punctuate the Muslim's entire life, from the age of puberty until death, are constituted of verses and chapters from the Quran, while Islamic Law has its root in the sacred text. Likewise, all branches of knowledge that can be legitimately called Islamic have their root in the Quran, which has served over the centuries as both the fountainhead and the guiding principle for the whole of the Islamic intellectual tradition.

The Quran was at first an aural revelation before becoming written in book form. The Prophet first *heard* the Word of God and then uttered it to his companions, who memorized the verses and wrote them on parchments, camel bones, and skins. According to the Islamic tradition, the Prophet was unlettered *(al-ummī)*, which on the highest level means that his soul was pure and virginal, undefiled by human knowledge and worthy of receiving the Divine Word. When the archangel Gabriel first appeared to the Prophet, the sound of the first verse of the Quran reverberated throughout the space around him. This aspect of the reality of the Quran remains very much alive to this day. Not only is the Quran a book written often in the most beautiful calligraphy and read throughout one's life, but it is also a world of sacred sound heard constantly in Islamic cities and towns. Its sounds reverberate throughout the spaces within which men and women move and act in their everyday lives, and there are many who have memorized the text and recite it constantly without reference to the written word. The art of chanting the Quran, which goes back to the Prophet, is the supreme acoustic sacred art of Islam and moves devout Muslims to tears whether they are Arabs or Malays.

As for the written text, it was the response of the soul of Muslims to the Quranic revelation that created the art of calligraphy, which was closely associated with the text of the Quran from the beginning and which constitutes, along with architecture, the supreme plastic sacred art of Islam. Architecture itself is a sacred art because it grows from and finds its highest expression in the architecture of the mosque, whose very spaces are defined by the reverberations of the recitation and chanting of the Quran.

The text of the Quran consists of 114 chapters *(sūrahs)* divided into the Meccan and the Medinan, that is, those revealed to the Prophet when he was in Mecca and those after he migrated to Medina. The very first verses revealed are those of the chapter entitled "Bloodclot" *(al-'Alaq)*, which open chapter 96 of the Quran. These verses are as follows:

In the Name of Allah, the Infinitely Good, the
All-Merciful
Recite in the Name of thy Lord who created!
He created man from a clot of blood.

Recite; and thy Lord is the Most Bountiful,
He who hath taught by the pen,
taught man what he knew not.[5]

The first chapter of the Quran is, however, the *ṣūrat al-fāṭihah*, "Chapter of the Opening," which consists of seven verses *(āyāt)*. It is without doubt the most often recited chapter of the Quran, because it constitutes the heart of the daily canonical prayers and contains, in a synoptic fashion, the message of the whole of the Quran:

In the Name of Allah, the Infinitely Good, the
All-Merciful
Praise be to God, the Lord of the worlds,
The Infinitely Good, the All-Merciful,
Master of the day of judgement.
Thee we worship, and in Thee we seek help.
Guide us upon the straight path,
the path of those on whom Thy grace is,
not those on whom Thy anger is,
nor those who are astray.[6]

The place of the chapters of the Quran is not based on the chronological order of their revelation, but on an order given by the Prophet, through Divine guidance, although it may be said that usually the longer chapters precede the shorter ones.

The content of the Quran varies greatly and covers a range of subjects from ethics to cosmology and metaphysics. According to Islamic teachings, the Quran contains the roots, or principles, of knowledge pertaining to both the domain of action and that of intellection and contemplation. It contains ethical and legal teachings as well as metaphysical ones pertaining to the Nature of God, cosmological ones related to the nature of His creation, and psychological ones concerning the human soul. It also bears a knowledge that pertains to the inner, spiritual life and to eschatological realities that concern the final ends of the individual and of human and cosmic history. The Quran also contains a sacred history, much of which it shares with the Bible, although it is not derived from the latter historically. The function of sacred history in the Quran is not so much to describe the outward history of the prophets of old, but rather to make vivid the reality of the continual battle within the human soul between the forces of good and evil, between knowledge and ignorance. The Quran also possesses a spiritual presence, an impalpable sacred reality that transforms the soul and is like a Divine net cast into the world of multiplicity to lead us back to the world of Unity.

For Muslims, everything about the Quran is sacred—its sounds, the very words of the Arabic language chosen by God to express His message, the letters in which it is written, and even the parchment or paper that constitutes the physical aspect of the sacred text. Muslims carry the Quran with full awareness of its sacred reality and usually do not touch it unless they have made their ablutions and are ritually clean.

They kiss it and pass under it when going on a journey, and many carry a small copy of it with them at all times for protection. The Quran is that central sacred presence that determines all aspects of Muslim life and the source and fountainhead of all that can be authentically called Islamic.

THE QURANIC SCIENCES AND COMMENTARIES ON THE QURAN

Many traditional sciences are associated with the Quran. First of all there is the art and science of recitation of the Quran, which is based on strict traditional sources that have been preserved and transmitted from generation to generation over the centuries. One cannot recite or chant the Quran in any way one wants. The very pauses and intonations are determined according to traditions going back to the Prophet. Another science studies the conditions under which particular verses were revealed *(sha'n al-nuzūl)* in order to understand better the intention of the text. Philological sciences are concerned with the study of the language of the Quran, which is so significant that it has determined the characteristics of classical Arabic for the past fourteen centuries. Classical Arabic is often taught, quite rightly, as Quranic Arabic in many Western universities. The serious study of the Arabic language and grammar is inseparable from the philological study of the

Quran, which gave rise historically, to a large extent, to the codification and systematization of Arabic grammar.

Perhaps the most important aspect of Quranic studies, however, concerns the deciphering of its meaning, or what is traditionally called *tafsīr* and *ta'wīl*, the former referring to the outward meaning of the text and the latter to its inner meaning. The science of Quranic commentary is one of the most important of the religious disciplines taught to this day in traditional Islamic schools. Quranic commentaries range from those concerned primarily with the language and grammar of the Quran, such as that of al-Zamakhsharī, to those concerned mostly with sacred history, like the *tafsīr* of al-Ṭabarī, to primarily theological commentaries, such as the immense *tafsīr* of Fakhr al-Dīn al-Rāzī. Islamic savants from practically every category have written commentaries on the Quran, including some of the most famous Islamic philosophers, such as Ibn Sīnā and Mullā Ṣadrā. Moreover, the tradition of writing Quranic commentaries continued unabated into the twentieth century with such notable *tafsīrs* as those of Mawlānā Abu'l-Kalām Āzād, Mawlānā Mawdūdī, Sayyid Quṭb, and 'Allāmah Ṭabāṭabā'ī, all of which deal not only with traditional questions, but also with many of the challenges and problems of the modern world in light of the teachings of the Quran.

Quranic commentaries that deal with the inner or esoteric meaning of the Quran *(ta'wīl)* were written mostly by Sufis and Shī'ites and go back to the famous commentary of Imām Ja'far al-Ṣādiq, both a pole (central spiritual authority) of Sufism and the sixth Shī'ite Imām. Over the centuries numerous Sufis have provided such commentaries, from al-Tustarī in the fourth/tenth century to Ibn 'Arabī in the seventh/thirteenth century and up to those in the present period; also included are many works in Persian, such as the vast commentary of Mībudī. Such a celebrated work of Sufism as the *Mathnawī* of Rūmī is in reality an esoteric commentary on the Quran according to the author himself. These commentaries deal with the inner meaning of various verses and even letters of the Quran, which have their own symbolic significance and are of prime importance in the development of Islamic metaphysics and cosmology. Shī'ite commentaries, too, have usually been concerned with the inner meaning of the sacred text in relation to the reality of the Imām, who is for them the interpreter par excellence of the inner dimension of the Word of God. In the climate of Shī'ism, some of the most important commentaries, such as that of al-Ṭabarsī, have been written by the *'ulamā'*, or official religious scholars, but many others have been written by those who were also philosophers and theosophers. The extensive commentaries of Mullā Ṣadrā are the prime example of this latter category.

The text of the Quran has been rendered often into English and numerous other European and non-European languages, although in its total reality the Quran is inimitable and untranslatable. Some of the translations have succeeded in conveying something of the poetic power of the original Arabic and others some of the external meanings. But no translation has been able or ever will be able to render the full meaning and "presence" of the text, which has many levels of interpretation and symbolic significance associated with the sound and structure of the words in the Arabic language and often the very form of Arabic letters. The Quranic commentaries could be guides for the understanding of at least some aspects of both outward and hidden, or symbolic, meanings of the text, but very few of them have been translated so far into English or other European languages.

The Prophet: His Significance, Life, and Deeds

The Prophet does not play the same role in Islam that Christ does in Christianity. He is not God incarnate or the God-man. Rather, he is human *(al-bashar)*, as asserted explicitly by the Quran, but unlike ordinary human beings in that he possesses the most perfect of natures, being, as a famous Arabic poem asserts, like a jewel among stones. The Prophet is seen by Muslims as the most perfect of all of God's creatures, the perfect man par excellence *(al-insān al-kāmil)* and the beloved of God *(ḥabīb Allāh)*, whom the Quran calls an excellent model *(uswah ḥasanah)* to emulate. He represents perfect surrender to God combined with proximity *(qurb)* to Him, which makes him the best interpreter of God's message as well as its most faithful transmitter. God gave him the most perfect character and embellished his soul with the virtues of humility, generosity or nobility, and sincerity in the highest degree, virtues that characterize all Islamic spirituality as it has become realized in the souls of Muslim men and women over the centuries.

Islam is based on the Absolute, Allah, and not on the messenger. Yet the love of the Prophet lies at the heart of Islamic piety, for human beings can love God only if God loves them, and God loves only the person who loves His Prophet. The Quran itself orders human beings to venerate the Prophet: "Lo! Allah and His angels shower blessings upon the Prophet. O ye who believe! Ask blessings upon him *(ṣallu)* and salute him *(sallimu)* with a worthy salutation" (33:56). This is the only act whose performance human beings share with God and the angels. Traditional Muslims therefore revere the Prophet in an inviolable manner and always ask for blessings *(ṣalāh)* and salutations *(salām)* upon him. In Muslim eyes, the love and respect for the Prophet are inseparable from the love for the Word of God, for the Quran, and of course ultimately for God Himself. There is something of the soul of the Prophet present in the Quran, and in a famous saying uttered before his death, the Prophet asserted that he was leaving two precious heritages behind for his community, the Quran and his family, both of which represent his continued presence in the Islamic community.

In Sufism and many schools of Islamic philosophical thought, the inner reality of the Prophet, the "Muḥammadan Reality" *(al-Ḥaqīqat al-muḥammadiyyah)*, is identified with the Logos, God's first creation, which is the ontological principle of creation as well as the archetype of all prophecy. Sufis assert that the inner reality of the Prophet was the first link in the prophetic chain and that his outward and historical reality came at the end of the prophetic cycle to bring it to a close. It was in reference to this inner reality that the Prophet asserted, "I was a prophet when Adam was between water and clay."

The love of the Prophet permeates all dimensions of Islam, affecting both those who follow the *Sharīʿah* and those who walk upon the spiritual path, the *Ṭarīqah*, of which he is the founder and guide. This love helps individual Muslims to emulate his habits and example, which constitute, along with the Quran, the foundation of Islamic Law. It also helps them to exert greater effort *(jihād)* to embellish their souls with the virtues and perfections that are to be found in their fullness in the person of the Prophet, whose life remains a model for every generation of Muslims.

The Prophet, who has many names and titles, including Muḥammad, Aḥmad, Muṣṭafā, and Abu'l-Qāsim,[7] was born in the full light of history in the city of Mecca in Arabia in 570 C.E. in the powerful tribe of Quraysh and the branch of Banū Hāshim. Mecca was at that time a major commercial and social center and also the religious heart of Arabia, for it was here that the various Arab tribes that had fallen into idolatry kept their idols at the Kaʿbah, the shrine built by Abraham to commemorate the One God. Arabia lived at that time in the "Age of Ignorance" *(al-jāhiliyyah)*, having forgotten the message of Unity associated with the father of monotheism, Abraham, who had visited Mecca and who is the father of the Arabs through his son Ismāʿīl (Ishmael). Yet a number of those who preserved the primordial monotheism survived, the people the Quran calls the *ḥunafā'* ("followers of the primordial religion"). The young Muḥammad never practiced idolatry, but was always faithful to the One God even before he was chosen as prophet.

He lost both parents at an early age and was brought up by his grandfather, 'Abd al-Muṭṭalib, and uncle, Abū Ṭālib, who was the father of 'Alī. He also spent some time among the bedouins in the desert outside Mecca. He soon gained the respect of everyone because of his great trustworthiness and came to be known as al-Amīn, "the Trusted One." At the age of twenty-five he married Khadījah, a wealthy businesswoman and widow some fifteen years older than he, who trusted him with guiding her caravans through the desert up to Syria. Khadījah, his first wife, bore him several children, including Fāṭimah, who married 'Alī and who is the mother of all the descendants of the Prophet, known as *sayyids* or *sharīfs*. The Prophet had a very happy family life with Khadījah and did not marry any other woman as long as she was alive. She was to provide great comfort and support for him, especially when he received the call of prophecy and was confronted with the very harsh treatment and enmity of the Meccans, including members of his own tribe.

The great event of revelation occurred in the life of the Prophet when he was forty years of age. He had always been contemplative and would often retreat into the desert to fast and pray. Once, when he was performing one of these retreats in the cave of al-Ḥirā' outside Mecca, the archangel Gabriel appeared to him, bringing him the first verses of the revelation that changed his life and that of much of the world dramatically. The revelation continued for the next twenty-three years, until the end of his life.

The verses of the Quran descended on the Prophet at different times and under different conditions until the revelation was completed shortly before his death. At first he doubted the reality of his experience, but soon the true nature of what he had received became evident. His first converts were his wife, Khadījah, his revered friend Abū Bakr, and his young cousin 'Alī. Gradually his circle of followers expanded to include his uncle Ḥamzah and some of the most eminent personages of Mecca, such as 'Umar ibn al-Khaṭṭāb. This success in turn increased the pressure of the Quraysh against him, for the new message implied nothing less than a complete change of their way of life, including the destruction of idols and idol worship, upon which their power rested. They finally decided to kill the Prophet, but God had planned otherwise. A delegation from a city to the north named Yathrib had come to Mecca and invited the Prophet to migrate *(al-hijrah)* to their city and become their ruler. The Prophet accepted their invitation and set out for that city in June 622. This date is so important for Islamic history that it marks the beginning of the Islamic calendar. It was in this city, soon to be named *Madīnat al-nabī*, "the City of the Prophet," or simply Medina, that Islam was to become for the first time a social and political order, one that would eventually expand into one of the major civilizations of the world.

In Medina, the Prophet became the ruler of a community; he was at once statesman, judge, and military leader as well as the Prophet of God. The newly founded community was threatened by the Meccans, who attacked it on several occasions in battles of crucial significance for Islamic history. These battles—Badr, Khandaq, Khaybar, and others—were all won by the Muslims despite their being greatly outnumbered (the exception was the battle of Uḥud, in which the Meccans left the field thinking that the Muslims had been completely defeated). Thereafter, the survival of the new community was assured. Meanwhile, tribes gradually came from all over Arabia to pay allegiance to the Prophet and accept the new religion, until finally the Meccans themselves could no longer resist. The Prophet marched into Mecca triumphantly in the year 8/630, forgiving all his enemies with great nobility and magnanimity. This episode marked, in a sense, the highlight of his earthly life—even his most ardent enemies embraced Islam. The Quran refers to this occasion in chapter 60:

> *In the Name of Allah, the Infinitely Good, the All-Merciful*
> *When Allah's succour, and triumph cometh and thou seest mankind entering the religion of Allah in troops,*
> *Then hymn the praise of thy Lord, and seek forgiveness of Him. Lo! He is ever ready to show mercy.*

The Prophet returned to Medina, from which he completed the Islamization of Arabia to the north. In the tenth year of the migration, he returned to Mecca to make the greater pilgrimage *(al-ḥajj)*, instituting the rites of *ḥajj* that continue to be performed to this day. That was also to be his farewell pilgrimage, for on returning to Medina he soon fell ill and after three days of illness died on the thirteenth of Rabīʿ al-awwal of the year 11/632. He was buried in the apartment of ʿĀʾishah, one of his wives whom he loved dearly, next to the mosque that was the first to be built in Islam. To this day his tomb stands at the center of the vast "mosque of the Prophet," and Medina remains the second holiest city of Islam, after Mecca.

In a twenty-three-year period, the Prophet succeeded in not only uniting Arabia under the banner of Islam, but also establishing a religious community of global extent, for which he remains always the ideal model of human behavior and action, and his biography *(al-Sīrah)* has remained a spiritual and religious guide for Muslims throughout the centuries. His extraordinary life included almost every possible human experience, which he was able to sanctify and integrate into the Islamic perspective. He experienced poverty, oppression, and cruelty as well as power and dominion. He tasted great love as well as the tragedy of the death of his beloved wife Khadījah and his only son. He lived in great simplicity, yet ruled over a whole cosmic sector. He lived with a single wife much older than he was until the age of fifty and then contracted many marriages in his later years, which proves precisely that his multiple marriages had nothing to do with passions of the flesh. In fact, most of them were for political reasons, to unite various tribes within the Islamic community. They also represent the sacred character of sexuality in Islam and a perspective on sexuality very different from the one that identifies it with original sin.

The supreme inner experience of the Prophet occurred in Mecca when one night, shortly before his migration to Medina, he was taken miraculously by the archangel Gabriel to Jerusalem and from there to the Presence of God in what is known as the Nocturnal Ascension *(al-mi'rāj)*. This experience, mentioned in the Quran, constitutes the inner reality of the daily prayers and the model for all spiritual ascent and realization in Islam. When we think of the life of the Prophet in its totality, we must not only think of him as the leader of a human community, a father and head of a family, a man who married several wives, or a ruler who participated in battles or made social and political decisions for the preservation of Islam. We must also meditate on his inner life of prayer, vigil, and fasting and especially the *mi'rāj*, for the Prophet and, with him, Islam came into the world to create a balance between the outward and the inward, the physical and the spiritual, and to establish an equilibrium on the basis of which human beings are able to realize the Unity, or *al-tawḥīd*, that is the goal of human life.

In the realization of this Unity, the model of the Prophet plays a basic role. That is why his wonts and deed, known in Arabic as *al-Sunnah*, are so central to the whole of Islam. The way he dressed and ate, the manner in which he treated his family and neighbors, his juridical and political deeds, and even his treatment of animals and plants constitute elements of his *Sunnah,* which is the most important source of Islam after the Quran. The *Sunnah* has been transmitted both orally and in written form over the centuries, and countless Muslims over the ages have sought to live and act in emulation of it. Its most direct expression is the *Ḥadīth,* or collection of sayings of the Prophet, which embrace practically every aspect of human life and thought.

THE *ḤADĪTH* AND ITS CODIFICATION

Since the *Ḥadīth* forms a major foundation of Islam, it is only natural that a great deal of attention has been devoted to it from the beginning. The earliest traces of written texts of the *Ḥadīth* are found in the edicts, letters, and treatises dictated by the Prophet himself, followed by his sayings recorded in the "pages" *(ṣaḥīfah)* of his Companions and the next generation, usually known as the Followers, or the *tābiʿūn.* This genre was followed by the class of texts known as "Documents" *(al-musnad),* by such scholars as Abū Dā'ūd al-Tayālisī. The most famous of this genre is that associated with the name of Imām Aḥmad ibn Ḥanbal, the founder of one of the four schools of Sunni Law, who died in the middle of the third/ninth century. One needs to mention here also the celebrated *al-Muwaṭṭa'* of Imām Mālik ibn Anas, the founder of another of the major schools of Sunni Law, who lived some half century before Imām Aḥmad ibn Ḥanbal and whose work many consider the first major collection of *Ḥadīth*, although the treatise deals primarily with jurisprudence *(al-fiqh)* and with *Ḥadīth* in relation to it.

All of these works as well as numerous other categories of writings were integrated into the major books of *Ḥadīth*, which appeared in the Sunni world in the third/ninth century. These great compendia, which are usually known as "The Six Correct Books" *(al-Ṣiḥāḥ al-sittah)* and constitute the canonical and orthodox sources of *Ḥadīth* in the Sunni world, are the *Jāmi' al-ṣaḥīḥ* of Abū 'Abd Allāh al-Bukhārī, the *Ṣaḥīḥ* of Abu'l-Ḥusayn ibn Muslim al-Nayshābūrī, the *Sunan* of Abū Dā'ūd al-Sijistānī, the *Jāmi'* of Abū 'Īsā al-Tirmidhī, the *Sunan* of Abū Muḥammad al-Dārimī, and the *Sunan* of Abū 'Abd Allāh ibn Mājah. There have been other important compilations, but they never gained the authority of these six works.

The great scholars of *Ḥadīth* carefully examined all the chains of transmission *(isnād)* of each saying, drawing on many other religious sciences, to sift the authentic sayings from those of dubious authority and both from sayings attributed to the Prophet but lacking any historical basis. Al-Bukhārī is said to have traveled widely from city to city and to have consulted more than a thousand authorities on *Ḥadīth*. Muslim scholarship had already created detailed criteria for evaluating the authenticity of each *ḥadīth* more than a millennium before Western orientalists appeared on the scene to deny the authenticity of the whole corpus. Needless to say, denying the whole corpus of *Ḥadīth* in effect invalidates the Islamic tradition itself. Obviously, the so-called historical criticism of such

Western scholars is not taken seriously by traditional Muslim scholars, especially since many of the Western orientalists' arguments have been negated by the discovery of recent historical evidence, while their whole position is implicitly based on the disavowal of the reality of Islamic revelation.

In the Shī'ite world, the corpus of *Ḥadīth* was collected and classified a century later than in the Sunni world and was based on the Shī'ites' own chain of transmission centered mostly on the family of the Prophet *(ahl al-bayt)*, although most of the *ḥadīths* are the same. The Shī'ite canonical collections consist of "The Four Books" *(al-Kutub al-arbaʻah)*: the *Uṣūl al-kāfī* of Muḥammad ibn Yaʻqūb al-Kulaynī, the *Man lā yaḥḍuruhu'l-faqīh* of Muḥammad ibn Bābūyah al-Qummī, and the *Kitāb al-istibṣār* and *Kitāb al-tahdhīb*, both by Muḥammad al-Ṭūsī. It is important to point out that in the Sunni world the term *ḥadīth* refers exclusively to a saying of the Prophet and a book of *Ḥadīth* to a collection of such sayings; in the Shī'ite world, however, a distinction is made between a "Prophetic saying" *(al-ḥadīth al-nabawī)* and a "saying of one of the Imāms" *(al-ḥadīth al-walawī)*, which is also highly prized and considered a kind of extension of the Prophetic *Ḥadīth*.

The *Ḥadīth* deals with nearly every human question, from details of legal significance to the most exalted moral and spiritual teachings. One *ḥadīth* asserts: "God is beautiful and He loves beauty," and another: "Verily there are heavenly rewards for any act of kindness to animals." Some *ḥadīths* deal with spiritual virtues and moral attitudes, such as: "Charity that is concealed appeaseth the wrath of God" and "God loveth those who are content." Much of the *Ḥadīth* deals with self-control, such as: "The most excellent *jihād* [usually translated "holy war," but literally meaning "exertion"] is that of the conquest of self" or "Whoever suppresseth his anger, when he hath in his power to show it, God will bestow upon him a great reward." Many other *ḥadīths* deal with duty toward others, such as "When the bier of anyone passeth by thee, whether Jew, Christian or Muslim, rise to thy feet" and "Abuse no one, and if a man abuse thee, and lay open a vice which he knoweth in thee; then do not disclose one which thou knowest in him."[8]

Altogether the *Ḥadīth* is a vast body of sayings concerning both the outer and inner dimensions of existence, the plane of action and that of contemplation, all of human life and every aspect of thought inasmuch as they pertain to the Islamic universe. The *Ḥadīth* reveals both the grandeur of the soul of the Prophet and his function as the supreme interpreter of God's Word and the prime exemplar for every Muslim. The *Ḥadīth* is a key for the comprehension of the attitudes and tendencies of the Muslim soul and the indispensable guide for the understanding of God's Word as contained in the Quran.

Among the thousands of *ḥadīths* of the Prophet are a small number that are called "sacred sayings" *(al-aḥādīth al-qudsiyyah)*; in them God speaks in the first person through the Prophet although they are not part of the Quran. This category of *ḥadīths* refers exclusively to the inner life and constitutes a very important source of Sufism. The definition of Sufism as the attainment of inner spiritual virtue *(iḥsān)* is in fact contained in one of the most famous of these sacred sayings: "*Iḥsān* is that thou adorest God as though thou didst see Him, and if thou seest Him not, He nonetheless seeth thee." These sayings dealing with the most inward and intimate aspects of the spiritual life have echoed over the centuries within the works of numerous Sufis who have meditated and commented on them. Having issued directly from God, they, therefore, constitute an indispensable source of that inner dimension of Islam that for the most part crystallized and became known as Sufism.

3

Doctrines and Beliefs of Islam

God

The central doctrine of Islam concerns God as He is in Himself as well as His Names and Qualities. The plenary doctrine of the nature of the Divinity as at once the Absolute, the Infinite, and the Perfect Good lies at the heart of the teachings of Islam. The Supreme Reality, or Allah (which, it must be recalled, is the Arabic word for God used by Christian Arabs and Arabized Jews as well as Muslims), is at once God, the Person, and the suprapersonal Reality or Godhead. Allah is not only Pure Being, but the Beyond-Being, about which nothing can be said without delimiting His Infinite and Absolute Essence, which is beyond all determination. That is why the *shahādah, Lā ilāha illa'Llāh* ("There is no god but God"), which contains the full Islamic doctrine of the nature of God, begins with the negative prefix *lā,* for to assert anything of the

Divine Essence or God in His or Its Supreme Reality is to limit It by that very assertion. Hence the Quranic verse: "There is nothing whatsoever like unto Him" (42:2).

Allah is the Absolute, the One, totally transcendent and beyond every limitation and boundary, every concept and idea. And yet He is also the Immanent, for, according to the Quran, "He is the First and the Last and the Outward and the Inward and He knows infinitely all things" (57:3). God is the First *(al-Awwal)*, for He is the Origin, the alpha, of all things. He is the Last *(al-Ākhir)*, for it is to Him that all things, not only human souls but the whole of the cosmos, return. He is the Outward *(al-Ẓāhir)*, for manifestation is ultimately nothing other than the theophany of His Names and Qualities on the tablet of "nothingness," and all existence is ultimately a ray of His Being. But He is also the Inward *(al-Bāṭin)*, for He is immanent in all things. Only the sage is able to understand and know, in the fullest sense of these terms, that God is the Immanent as well as the Transcendent and to completely grasp the sense of the verse: "Whithersoever ye turn, there is the Face of God" (2:115). Moreover, the sage can gain this understanding only by virtue of his or her having realized the Divine Transcendence *(ta'ālī)*, for the Divine reveals itself as the Immanent only by virtue of having been first known and experienced as the Transcendent.

God possesses an Essence *(al-Dhāt)* that is beyond all categories and definitions, like that darkness which is dark because of the intensity of its luminosity, the black light to which certain Sufis have referred. Although beyond all duality and gender, the Divine Essence is often referred to in the feminine form, and *al-Dhāt* is of feminine gender in Arabic. In Its aspect of infinitude It is, metaphysically speaking, the supreme principle of femininity, standing above and beyond the aspect of the Divinity as Creator while in Its aspect of absoluteness It is the principle of masculinity. Furthermore, the Essence delimits Itself in the Divine Names and Qualities that constitute the very principles of cosmic manifestation and are the ultimate archetypes of all that exists, both macrocosmically and microcosmically. The Quran asserts: "To God belong the most beautiful Names; call Him by these Names" (7:180). The science of the Divine Names lies at the heart of all Islamic intellectual and religious disciplines—metaphysics as well as cosmology, theology as well as ethics—and plays a central role in the practical aspects of religion and religious worship through the invocation and recitation of the Divine Names, including the Supreme Name, *Allāh*, particularly in Sufism.

The Names of God in Islam were revealed and sanctified by God Himself through the Quranic revelation, hence their power to return human beings to their Origin. The Supreme Name refers to both the Divine Essence and the Divine Qualities and contains all the Names. There are traditionally ninety-nine Names of God, hence the ninety-nine beads of the Islamic rosary. These are all sacred Names in Arabic chosen by God as He has revealed Himself in Islam. They are made known to Muslims through the Quran and *Ḥadīth*. These Names are divided into the Names of Perfection *(asmā' al-kamāl)*, the Names of Majesty *(asmā' al-jalāl)*, and the Names of Beauty *(asmā' al-jamāl)*, the last two being, respectively, the principles of the masculine and the feminine as manifested throughout the cosmic order.

God is both merciful and just. He is *al-Raḥmān* ("the Infinitely Good"), *al-Raḥīm* ("the All-Merciful"), *al-Karīm* ("the Generous"), *al-Ghafūr* ("the Forgiver"), and so on. But He is also *al-Qahhār* ("the Ever-Dominant"), *al-ʿĀdil* ("the Just"), *al-Mumīt* ("the Giver of Death"), and *al-Muntaqim* ("the Avenger"). The universe and all that is in it are woven of the theophanies and reflections of the Divine Names, which, as already mentioned, play a central role in both Islamic thought and piety. Together, they reveal one of the most complete doctrines of the nature of the Supreme Divinity in any religion. It seems that through them the One God of Abraham finally revealed the fullness of His Face.

Prophecy and Revelation

Islam asserts that after the doctrine of Divine Oneness, or the doctrine concerning the nature of God *(al-tawḥīd)*, the most important doctrine is that of prophecy *(nubuwwah)*. According to Islamic understanding, God has made prophecy the central reality of human history; the cycle of prophecy began with Adam and was brought to a close with the Quranic revelation. There are, moreover, 124,000 prophets, sent to every nation and people, and God has never left a people without revelation, as the Quran asserts explicitly: "Verily to every people there is a messenger" (10:48).

A prophet is chosen by God and by Him alone. Classes of prophets *(anbiyā')* range from those who bring some news from God *(nabī)* to messengers *(rasūl)* who bring major messages. And then there are the possessors of determination *(ūlu'l-'aẓm)*, like Moses, Jesus, and the Prophet of Islam, who established major new religions. In all cases, the prophet receives his message from God; his words and deeds are not the result of his own genius or historical borrowings. A prophet owes nothing to anyone save God. He brings a message that has the freshness and perfume of veritable originality because his message comes from the Origin, a message vis-à-vis which he remains the passive receiver and transmitter. Revelation *(al-waḥy)* in Islam is understood in the precise sense of reception of a message from Heaven through an angelic instrument of revelation without the interference of the human substance of the receiver, who is the prophet. It needs to be added, however, that the message is always revealed in forms that are in accordance with the world for which it is intended and with the earthly receptacle chosen by God for His particular message.

Understood in this sense, revelation is clearly distinguished from inspiration *(al-ilhām)*, which is possible for all human beings by virtue of their being human, but which is usually actualized only within those who prepare the mind and soul through spiritual practice for the reception of true inspiration. Of course, the "Spirit bloweth where it listeth," and inspiration can occur in circumstances that cannot always be understood by looking at only the external conditions and causes in question.

The Angelic World

The Quran refers constantly to the angels *(al-malā'ikah)*, and belief in their existence is part of the definition of faith *(al-īmān)*. Angels play a major role in the Islamic universe; they bring revelation, as was done by Jibra'īl (Gabriel), and take the soul of men and women at the moment of death, as is done by 'Izrā'īl. There is a vast hierarchy of angels, ranging from those who surround and support the Divine Throne *(al-'arsh)* to those who carry out the commands of God during everyday life in the world of nature. The angels are of course luminous and forces for the good, totally immersed in the beatitude of the Divine Presence and subservient to His Will. And yet the Devil, al-Iblīs, was also originally an angel who fell from grace and became the personification of evil because of his refusal to prostrate himself before Adam.

The angels play a basic role in Islamic cosmology as well as in philosophy, where some of them are identified as instruments of knowledge and illumination. They also play an important role in everyday religious life, where they are experienced as very real parts of the cosmos within which Muslims live. One can say that the angels have not as yet been banished from the religious cosmos of Muslims, as they have been to an ever greater degree in Western Christianity from the seventeenth century on. Angels must, however, be distinguished from the *jinn*, also mentioned in the Quran, who are psychic rather than spiritual forces, but who also inhabit the Islamic cosmos and play a role in the total economy of that cosmos.

The Human State

Islam considers man, that is, the human being in both the male and female forms, in himself and in his suchness as standing directly before God and being both His servant *(al-'abd)* and vicegerent *(al-khalīfah)* on earth. God created the first man (Adam) from clay and breathed His Spirit into him. He taught Adam the name of all things and ordered all the angels to prostrate themselves before him, which all except Satan did. To quote the Quranic verse: "And when we said unto the angels: Prostrate yourselves before Adam, they fell prostrate, all save Iblīs. He demurred through pride, and so became a disbeliever" (2:34). Some Muslim authorities say that God created Eve from Adam and others that they were both created from the same clay. In any case, God made Eve Adam's companion and complement, and the two resided in paradise until they disobeyed God's command by eating of the fruit of the forbidden tree. Henceforth they fell *(al-hubūṭ)* from paradisal perfection on earth and became tainted with the forgetfulness *(al-ghaflah)* that characterizes fallen human beings; but they did not commit original sin in the Christian sense, which would radically distort human nature. Furthermore, Adam and Eve were jointly responsible for their fall; it was not Eve who tempted Adam to eat of the forbidden fruit.

According to the Islamic perspective, men and women still carry deep within their souls that primordial nature *(al-fiṭrah)*, which attests to Divine Unity and which Islam essentially addresses. For Islam, the human being is an intelligence, which by nature confirms *al-tawḥīd*, and to this intelligence is added the will, which needs to be guided by revelation. The function of religion is to remove the veil of the passions, which prevent the intelligence from functioning correctly. Religion is essentially the means for men and women to recollect who they are and to return to the inner primordial nature they still carry deep within themselves.

Human beings must be perfectly passive toward Heaven as the servant or slave of God *('abd Allāh)*, and active toward the world around them as God's vicegerent on earth. To be truly human is to receive in perfect submission from God and to give to creation as the central channel of grace for the created order. Islam rejects completely the Promethean and Titanic conception of human beings as creatures in rebellion against Heaven, an idea that has come to largely dominate the Western concept of the human state since the Renaissance. In the Islamic perspective, the grandeur of men and women is not in themselves, but in their submission to God, and human grandeur is always judged by the degree of servitude toward God and His Will. Even the power given to human beings to both know and dominate things is legitimate only on the condition that they remember their theomorphic nature according to the *ḥadīth* "God created man upon His form" and continue to remain subservient to that blinding Divine Reality that is the ontological principle and ultimate goal of return of human beings. All human grandeur causes the Muslim soul to remember that *Allāhu akbar*, "God is greater," and that all grandeur belongs ultimately to Him.

Islam also sees human nature in its permanent reality as standing before God and reflecting like a mirror all of His Names and Qualities, while all other creatures reflect only one or some of His Names. The human creature as we know it now did not evolve from some lower form. Human beings have always been human beings and will always be so, and no evolution of the human state is possible. The human being is like the center of the circle of terrestrial existence. Once one is at the center of the circle, one cannot evolve or move any closer toward the center. During human history, the Divine Truth has shone or been eclipsed to various degrees, but human beings have always remained basically human beings, the beings whom God addresses directly in the Quran, making every Muslim, male and female, like a priest who stands directly before God and communicates with Him without the aid of any intermediary.

Man and Woman

Many Quranic verses address men and women separately, as distinct sexes, while others refer to the human species as such. The injunctions of Islam are meant for both men and women, both of whom have immortal souls, are held responsible for their actions in this world, and will be judged accordingly in the hereafter. The gates of both Heaven and hell as well as the intermediate purgatorial states are open to members of both sexes, and the injunctions of religion pertain to both men and women, who are equal before the Divine Law in this world and before God on the Day of Judgment.

As far as the social and economic aspects of life are concerned, Islam sees the role of the two sexes in their complementarity rather than in their opposition. The role of women is seen primarily but not necessarily exclusively as preserving the family and bringing up the children and that of men as protecting the family and providing economically for it. The Quran, however, does not forbid women to engage in economic or even political life, and in certain sectors of even traditional Islamic society, such as agriculture, women have always participated in economic life on a par with men. Both men and women have, however, complete economic independence according to Islamic Law, and a woman can do what she wants with her wealth independent of her husband. What is especially emphasized is the central role of the family, which remains very strong to this day in Islamic countries despite the fact that divorce is not forbidden in Islamic Law. According to a saying of the Prophet, of all the things permitted by God, that which He dislikes most is divorce.

Sexuality in Islam is considered sacred in itself; therefore, marriage is not a sacrament, but a contract made between the two parties. Polygamy is permitted only under certain condion the condition that they remain aware of their vicegerency, which brings with it responsibility toward all of God's creation.

The ecological and environmental disasters in many parts of the Islamic world today, especially in the big cities, must not be seen as the result of Islamic teachings any more than the terrible pollution in many parts of Japan can be considered the consequence of Zen Buddhism or Shinto teachings about nature. The traditional Islamic view of the cosmos and the natural order did not cause such disasters, but Islam created a civilization that lived in peace with nature for more than a millennium. Islam also developed a vast metaphysics, theology, and sacred science of nature; and in traditional art, even though it has never become naturalistic, nature as God's creation and reflection of His wisdom and power plays a central role. It is important to note in this connection that the Islamic paradise is not composed only of crystals; it is also populated by plants and animals. In fact, many of the animals and plants of this world directly reflect certain paradisal qualities here below.

Eschatology

Much of the Quran and many of the *ḥadīths* of the Prophet are concerned with eschatological, or end-time, realities, both microcosmic and macrocosmic. Islam believes that at death, individuals enter a state in conformity with their faith and

tions, including consent of all the parties concerned and just behavior toward the wives, but all sexual promiscuity is strictly forbidden and strongly punishable according to Islamic Law, although the punishment of adultery can take place only if there are four witnesses to the act. Most families in the Islamic world are monogamous, and the practice of polygamy, which is the exception rather than the rule, is usually dictated by economic and social factors and Islam's desire to see all members of society integrated into a family structure. When practiced according to Islamic teachings, polygamy is not legalized promiscuity, as some Western critics claim, but a way of seeing that men bear economic and social responsibility for all their mates and offsprings.

The Islamic conception of the complementarity of men and women and the sacred character of sexuality is also reflected in the separation of men and women in social situations and the meaning of the wearing of the veil. The latter is not unique to Islam; it has been practiced over the millennia by the Jewish and Christian populations of the East as well. Yet since it is emphasized by Islam, it is often identified in the Western mind with that religion alone. Islam demands modesty of dress for women; a woman is not to display her "ornaments," which has usually been interpreted as her body and hair, before strangers. The veiling of the face was an ancient pre-Islamic custom practiced in the sedentary centers of the Middle East that was adopted later by many Muslim women, although it is still not practiced by either nomadic or peasant Muslim women in smaller villages. The covering of women is also directly related to the interiorization that the female represents vis-à-vis the male. If one takes the total Islamic doctrine of the two sexes into consideration, one can say that the rapport between them is that of equality—superiority of the male over the female and the superiority of the female over the male—depending on whether one considers the metacosmic, cosmic, or the terrestrially human aspects of this relationship and duality. This relation has its roots in the complementarity of the Divine Names and, even beyond that domain, in the nature of the Divine in Itself as both absolute and infinite.

The Cosmos

The Quran refers constantly to the world of nature as well as to the human order. The sky and the mountains, the trees and animals in a sense participate in the Islamic revelation, through which the sacred quality of the cosmos and the natural order is reaffirmed. The sacred scripture of Islam refers to the phenomena of nature as *āyāt* ("signs" or "portents"), the same term used for its verses and the signs that appear within the soul of human beings according to the famous verse: "We shall show them our portents *(āyāt)* upon the horizons and within themselves, until it be manifest unto them that it is the Truth" (41:53). Natural phenomena are not only phenomena in the current understanding of the term. They are signs that

reveal a meaning beyond themselves. Nature is a book whose *āyāt* are to be read like the *āyāt* of the Quran; in fact, they can only be read thanks to the latter, for only revelation can unveil for fallen man the inner meaning of the cosmic text. Certain Muslim thinkers have referred to the cosmos as the "Quran of creation" or the "cosmic Quran" *(al-Qur'ān al-takwīnī)*, whereas the Quran that is read every day by Muslims is called the "recorded Quran" *(al-Qur'ān al-tadwīnī)*. The cosmos is the primordial revelation whose message is still written on the face of every mountain and tree leaf and is reflected through the light that shines from the sun, the moon, and the stars. But as far as Muslims are concerned, this message can only be read by virtue of the message revealed by "the recorded Quran."

In light of this perspective, Islam does not create an impenetrable wall between the natural and the supernatural. Divine grace, or *barakah*, flows both from the sacred rites and through the arteries of the universe, and natural elements play a major role in Muslim religious life. Islamic rites have an astronomical and cosmic dimension. The times of the daily prayers are determined by the actual movement of the sun, as are the beginning and end of the fast. The earth itself is the primordial mosque, and spaces of human-made mosques are themselves emulations and recapitulations of the space of virgin nature. Muslims have always traditionally lived in harmony with nature and in equilibrium with the natural environment, a harmony that can be clearly seen in the urban design of traditional Islamic cities. Human beings have always been seen as God's vicegerents and are permitted to dominate nature only

actions in this life, although there are always imponderable dimensions of Divine Mercy. The Quran and *Ḥadīth* describe vividly both paradise and hell and also point to the purgatories or intermediate states in between that have been described more fully in the inspired traditional commentaries. The language used, especially in the Quran, to describe eschatological realities is vivid and concrete; yet it is also symbolic and must not be understood only in its literal sense, although the literal sense also possesses significance on its own level. The depiction of posthumous states and eschatological realities, which are beyond the ken of human imagination, can be expressed only symbolically. The true meaning of these descriptions must be sought in the inspired commentaries and the sapiential writings of such figures as Ibn 'Arabī and Ṣadr al-Dīn Shīrāzī.

Islam also possesses an elaborate teaching concerning eschatological events on the macrocosmic level. For Islam, human and cosmic history have an end just as they have a beginning. The end of human history will be marked by the advent of the coming of a person named the Mahdī, who will destroy oppression, defeat the enemies of religion, and re-establish peace and justice on earth. The Sunnis believe the Mahdī to be a member of the tribe of the Prophet and bearing the name Muḥammad, while the Shī'ites identify him with the Twelfth Imām, Muḥammad al-Mahdī. In any case, both branches of Islam believe that the rule of the Mahdī will be followed, after a period known exactly only to God, by the return of Christ to Jerusalem, which will bring human history to a close and lead to the Day of Judgment. Christ plays a central role in Islamic eschatology, not as the Christian Christ who is a part of the Trinity, but as a major figure in the chain of Abrahamic prophets asserting the Oneness of God. The belief in the coming of the Mahdī is so strong that throughout Islamic history, especially during periods of oppression and turmoil, it has led to various millennialist movements, and many charismatic figures have appeared over the centuries claiming to be the Mahdī. Some of them have left an important mark on various regions of the Islamic world, as one sees in the case of the thirteenth/nineteenth-century Mahdī of the Sudan. In any case, belief in the coming of the Mahdī remains strong throughout the Islamic world, and the acceptance of the eschatological realities connected to the Day of Jugment is part and parcel of the Islamic credo; they remain a living reality for Muslims throughout their life here on earth, which is but a preparation for the meeting with God and the hereafter.

4

The Dimensions of Islam

Divine Law: Its Content, Codification, and Schools

The *Sharīʿah,* or Divine Law of Islam, not only is central to the religion, but also constitutes Islam itself in its ritual, legal, ethical, and social aspects. Muslims believe that the *Sharīʿah* contains the concrete embodiment of the Will of God, how God wants them to act in this life to gain happiness in this world and felicity in the hereafter. A Muslim can fail to practice the injunctions of the *Sharīʿah* and still remain a Muslim, although not a practicing and upright one, but if he or she no longer considers the *Sharīʿah* to be valid, then he or she practically ceases to be a Muslim. The life of the Muslim from the cradle to the grave is governed by the *Sharīʿah,* which sanctifies every aspect of life, creates equilibrium in human society, and provides the means for human beings to live virtuously and to fulfill their functions as God's creatures placed on earth to submit themselves to His Will and to live according to His laws. A Muslim may go beyond the outer meaning of the *Sharīʿah* and through the Path, or the *Ṭarīqah,* reach the Truth, or *Ḥaqīqah,* which resides within the sacred forms and injunctions of the Law, but he or she must start with the *Sharīʿah* and follow it to the best of his or her ability.

The *Sharīʿah* is like the circumference of a circle, each point of which represents a Muslim who stands on that circumference. Each radius that connects every point on the circumference to the center symbolizes the *Ṭarīqah,* and the center is the *Ḥaqīqah,* which generates both the radii and the circumference. The whole circle, with its center, circumference, and radii, may be said to represent the totality of the Islamic tradition. One can follow one of the radii to the center, but only on the condition of beginning on the circumference —hence, the great significance of the *Sharīʿah,* without which no spiritual journey would be possible and the religion itself could not be practiced. Furthermore, even the greatest saints and sages who have reached the *Ḥaqīqah* do not cease to practice the *Sharīʿah* throughout their earthly lives.

The word *Sharīʿah* comes from the root *shr*ʿ, which means "road," and the *Sharīʿah* is the road that men and women must follow in this life. Since Islam is a complete way of life, the *Sharīʿah* is all-embracing; it includes all of life from rites of worship to economic transactions. Usually, however, it is divided for the sake of clarification and to facilitate learning its injunctions into *ʿibādāt* (what pertains to worship) and *muʿāmalāt* (what pertains to transactions). In the first category are included all the injunctions that apply to Islamic rites, both the obligatory and the recommended, such as prayer and fasting; the second category includes every kind of transaction, whether it is social, economic, or political and whether it is concerned with one's neighbor or with the whole of society.

The *Sharī'ah* divides all acts into five categories: those that are obligatory *(wājib)*; those that are recommended *(mandūb)*; acts toward which the Divine Law is indifferent *(mubāḥ)*; acts that are reprehensible or abominable *(makrūh)*; and those that are forbidden *(ḥarām)*. An example of the first would be the daily prayers *(ṣalāh)*; of the second, giving money to the poor; of the third, the kind of vegetables one eats or exercise one performs; the fourth, divorce; and the fifth, murder, adultery, and theft as well as certain dietary prohibitions such as the consumption of pork and its derivatives or alcoholic beverages. Muslims live a life woven of actions whose evaluation is known to them on the basis of the *Sharī'ah*. That does not mean that Muslims have no freedom, for freedom is defined in Islam not simply as individual rebellion against all authority, but participation in that freedom that in its fullness belongs to God alone. Muslims gain freedom, not confinement, by conforming to the Divine Law, because the very boundaries of their being are expanded through such conformity. By surrendering to the Will of God, Muslims are able to transcend the imprisonment of their own egos and the stifling confinement of their passionate selves.

The roots of the *Sharī'ah* are found in the Quran, and God is considered the ultimate legislator *(al-Shāri')*. The *Ḥadīth* and *Sunnah*, however, complement the Quran as the second major source of the *Sharī'ah*, for the Prophet was the interpreter par excellence of the meaning of God's Word. From the very beginning, even in Mecca, but especially in the Medinan community, the *Sharī'ah* began to be promulgated through the actual practices of the Prophet and the nascent Islamic community and the pronouncements handed down by the Prophet as the judge of the newly founded Islamic society. On the basis of this early practice and the twin sources of the Quran and *Sunnah* (which includes the *Ḥadīth*)—and also the use of such principles as *ijmā'*, or consensus of the community, and *qiyās*, or analogy—later generations continued to apply and codify the Law until the second/eighth and third/ninth centuries, when the founders of the great schools of Law *(al-madhāhib)*, which have continued to this day, appeared on the scene. In the Sunni world these include Imām Mālik ibn Anas, Imām Abū Ḥanīfah, Imām Muḥammad al-Shāfi'ī, and Imām Aḥmad ibn Ḥanbal, after whom, respectively, the Mālikī, Ḥanafī, Shāfi'ī, and Ḥanbalī schools are named. Among these figures, Imām Shāfi'ī is especially remembered for developing the method of jurisprudence related to the major principles of the Quran, *Sunnah*, *ijmā'*, and *qiyās* as well as others, not all of which are accepted by all the schools of Law.

Today the vast majority of Sunnis continue to follow these schools: the North and West Africans are almost completely Mālikī; the Egyptians, Malays, and Indonesians almost all Shāfi'ī; the Turks and the Turkic people as well as the Sunnis of the Indo-Pakistani Subcontinent mostly Ḥanafī; and the Saudis and many Syrians Ḥanbalī. The school of Law of Twelve-Imām Shī'ism is called Ja'farī, named after Imām Ja'far al-Ṣādiq, who was the sixth Shī'ite Imām and also the teacher of Imām Abū Ḥanīfah. Together these five schools compose the major *madhāhib* of the *Sharī'ah.* There are, however, a few smaller schools, such as that of the Zaydīs, the Ismā'īlī Shī'ites, and the 'Ibādīs of Oman and southern Algeria. There were also other schools of Sunni Law that gradually died out and have no followers today.

These schools of the *Sharī'ah* represent different interpretations of the Law on the basis of the basic sources, but their differences are minor. Even between the four Sunni schools and Ja'farī Law, there are no major differences except that Ja'farī Law permits temporary marriage, which is forbidden in the four schools of Sunni Law, and emphasizes inheritance more in the line of the descendants, rather than the siblings, of a person. As for the basic rites, the differences between Sunnis and Shī'ites hardly exceed those between the various schools of Sunni Law.

The great jurists (*fuqahā'*, pl. of *faqīh)* who codified the schools of Law practiced the rendering of new opinions based on the basic sources, or what is called *ijtihād.* In the Sunni world the gate of *ijtihād* became closed in the fourth/tenth century, and many authorities have been seeking to open it since the end of the nineteenth century. In the Shī'ite world, the gate of *ijtihād* has always been open, and it is considered essential that in each generation those who have the qualifications to practice *ijtihād*, called *mujtahids,* go back to the

Quran, *Sunnah*, and *Ḥadīth* (which for Shīʿites includes the sayings of the Shīʿite Imāms) and reformulate in a fresh manner the body of the Law.

The *Sharīʿah* has immutable principles, but also contains the possibility of growth and application to whatever situation Muslims face. It must be remembered, however, that in the Islamic perspective law is not simply a human-made system created for convenience in a particular social context. Law is of Divine origin and must mold society according to its norms, not vice versa. To the assertion often made by modern Western critics of Islam that Islamic Law must keep up with the times, Islam answers that if this is so, then what must the times keep up with? What is it that orders or forces the times to change as they do? Islam believes that the factor to make the times and coordinate human society must be the *Sharīʿah.* Human beings must seek to live according to the Will of God as embodied in the *Sharīʿah* and not change the Law of God according to the changing patterns of a society based on the impermanence of human nature.

The Spiritual Path: The Sufi Orders and the Doctrinal and Practical Teachings of Sufism

The inner or esoteric *(al-bāṭin)* dimension of Islam became crystallized for the most part in Sufism, although elements of it can also be found in Shīʿism. Sufism, a word equivalent to the Arabic term *al-taṣawwuf*, is simply the teachings and practices related to the path leading directly to God *(al-ṭarīqah ila'Llāh)*. According to a *ḥadīth*, there are as many paths to God as there are children of Adam, and although, needless to say, an indefinite number of paths did not come into being, over time a large number of *ṭuruq* (pl. of *ṭarīqah*) did develop that were able to cater to different spiritual and psychological human types. Usually called Sufi orders, these paths have protected and promulgated the esoteric teachings of Islam to this day and still constitute a vital element in Islamic society.

Sufism is like the heart of the body of Islam, invisible from the outside but providing nourishment for the whole organism. It is the inner spirit that breathes in the outward forms of the religion and makes possible the passage from the outer world to the inward paradise—a paradise we carry in our heart at the center of our being but remain, for the most part, unaware of because of the hardening of the heart associated by Islam with the sin of forgetfulness *(al-ghaflah)*. Sufism provides the cure for this malady in the form of the balm of invocation *(al-dhikr)*, which is at once "remembrance," "mention," and "invocation," the quintessential prayer that becomes finally united with the heart, which according to Islam is the "Throne of the Compassionate" *('arsh al-raḥmān)*.

The whole of Sufism is based, on the one hand, on *al-dhikr*, the means of meditation, and action to facilitate the *dhikr*. On the other hand, it is based on the exposition of a knowledge of reality that at once prepares human beings for the journey to God, prepares the mind and soul for *dhikr*, and is the fruit of the path in the form of realized knowledge (*al-ma'rifah* or *'irfān*). In this path to God, human beings begin with the sense of reverence for and fear of God *(al-makhāfah)* in accordance with the *ḥadīth:* "The beginning of wisdom is the fear of God." They are then led to the love of God *(al-maḥabbah)*, concerning which the Quran asserts: "A people whom He loves and they love Him" (5:57). And the path is crowned by that illuminating knowledge, or gnosis *(al-ma'rifah)*, which in Sufism is never separated from love.

The prototype of Sufi life is the life of the Prophet, and no group throughout Islamic history has loved him as intensely and sought to emulate his wonts and deeds as fervently as Sufis. The virtues that Sufis extol and with which they seek to embellish their souls are those of the Prophet, whose Nocturnal Ascent, as already mentioned, is the prototype of all spiritual ascent and realizations in Sufism. The esoteric teachings of Islam were transmitted by him to a few of his companions. Foremost among them was 'Alī, who is the link between the Prophet and almost all of the Sufi orders in the initiatic chain *(al-silsilah)*, which relates every Sufi generation back to the Prophet. A few of the other companions, such as Abū Bakr and Salmān al-Fārsī, the first Persian to embrace Islam, also played an important role in the early history of this esoteric teaching, which began to be called *al-taṣawwuf* in the second/eighth century. The most important figure after this early generation, who connects its members to the Sufis of the second/eighth century, was the great patriarch of Basra, Ḥasan al-Baṣrī, who had many students, including the famous woman Sufi saint and poet from Basra, Rābi'ah al-'Adawiyyah.

Following the period of the Mesopotamian ascetics and Sufis that occurred immediately after Ḥasan, gradually two distinct schools of Sufism developed. These schools were associated with Baghdad and Khurasan, each of which produced many illustrious Sufis, the first being known more for its "sobriety" and the second for its "drunkenness." At this time Sufis gathered around individual masters, and their organization was quite loose and informal. The most famous circle of this kind in the third/ninth century was that of Junayd of Baghdad, who had numerous disciples, including the celebrated Manṣūr al-Ḥallāj, who was put to death as a result of political intrigue but on the specific charge of religious heresy for having uttered in public, "I am the Truth *(ana'l-Ḥaqq)*"—*al-Ḥaqq* being one of the Names of God. Khurasan also produced numerous masters whose fame has continued to this day, including the great saint Bāyazīd al-Basṭāmī. It was also from there that the intellectual defense of Sufism vis-à-vis the jurists, exoteric scholars, and theologians was to be carried out in the fifth/eleventh century by the famous Persian theologian and Sufi Abū Ḥāmid Muḥammad al-Ghazzālī. It was also the land from which Persian Sufi literature—a literature that changed the spiritual and religious landscape of much of Asia—was to rise, reaching its peak with Jalāl al-Dīn Rūmī in the seventh/thirteenth century.

From the fifth/eleventh century onward Sufism became more organized, and the Sufi orders, or *ṭuruq*, as we know them today, appeared on the scene. The earliest ones, the Qādiriyyah and the Rifā'iyyah, still exist today. The orders were and are usually named after their founder, who is able to establish a new order with its own regulations and practices on the basis of his God-given authority. Some of these orders, such as the Mawlawiyyah, founded by Rūmī, the Shādhiliyyah, by Shaykh Abu'l-Ḥasan al-Shādhilī, and the Naqshbandiyyah, by Shaykh Bahā' al-Dīn Naqshband, all in the seventh/thirteenth and eighth/fourteenth centuries, have had a geographically widespread following. Others, such as the Aḥmadiyyah order in Egypt and the Ni'matullāhiyyah order in Persia, have been confined to a large extent to a particular land, at least until recently.

A Sufi order consists of a hierarchy, at the head of which resides the spiritual master, usually known as *shaykh* or *pīr* (in Persian and many Eastern languages used by Muslims). He or she has representatives of various ranks who run the affairs of the order and in some cases provide spiritual advice and have permission to initiate people into the order. Disciples are usually called *murīd* (the person who has the will to follow the spiritual path), *faqīr* (literally "the poor," meaning the person who realizes that he or she is poor and all richness belongs to God), or *darwīsh* (a Persian term meaning "humble" or "lowly"). In Arabic and Persian, Sufis do not usually call themselves "Sufis"—the term *ṣūfī* being reserved for those who have already reached the end of the path. The disciple is initiated by the *shaykh* or one of his or her authorized representatives according to a rite that goes back to the Prophet. Henceforth, the disciple follows the spiritual path under the direction of the guide with the goal of reaching God, becoming "annihilated" and effaced *(al-fanā')* in His Infinite Reality, and gaining subsistence *(al-baqā')* in Him.

The path may be said to consist of three elements: a doctrine concerning the nature of Reality; a method to reach the Real; and a science or alchemy of the soul dealing with embellishing the soul with virtue and removing from it all the imperfections or veils that prevent it from becoming wed to the Spirit. This last element can also be described using another Sufi symbol: removing the opacity or the veils that prevent the "eye of the heart" *('ayn al-qalb* or *chism-i dil)* from seeing God and viewing everything as a theophany of God. The doctrine is ultimately always a commentary on the two *shahādahs*, although in later Islamic history it became elaborated into a vast metaphysical edifice, especially in the hands of the seventh/thirteenth-century master of Islamic gnosis Muḥyī al-Dīn ibn 'Arabī. Over the centuries Sufis have provided the profoundest metaphysics, cosmology, angelology, psychology, and eschatology to be found in the Islamic tradition and one of the most complete metaphysical expositions found in any religious tradition. In the expounding of these doctrines, they have drawn at times from the formulations of Neoplatonism, Hermeticism, and ancient Iranian and in some cases Indian teachings, but the central truth of their doctrine has remained the doctrine of Unity *(al-tawḥīd)* and the teachings of the Quran, whose inner meaning they have expounded in their many works.

As for method, the central means of attachment to the Real is the *dhikr*. Each order has its own particular methods of meditation and litanies devised by the master of the order according to the need of the adepts. Because all Sufi orders constantly emphasize the third element, the science of the soul and the cultivation of the virtues, it often appears that Sufism is nothing but the cultivation of spiritualized virtues. In a sense the metaphysical knowledge and the method belong to God. The adept's contribution is his or her attainment of the virtues and the use of his or her will to constantly combat the negative and passionate tendencies of the soul, until, with the help of the method and the "Muḥammadan grace" *(al-barakat al-muḥammadiyyah)*, the lead of the soul becomes transmuted into gold, and the heavy substance of the carnal soul, which, when left to itself, falls down like a rock, becomes transformed into an eagle that flies upward toward the supernal sun. But it must be remembered that even the virtues in the deepest sense belong to God. What alone belongs to human beings is their awareness of their "nothingness" before Him.

Sufism has played and continues to play a central role in the Islamic tradition. It has played a major role in the intellectual life of Islam and has interacted with both theology and philosophy in numerous ways over the centuries. It has been a fountainhead for Islamic art, and many of the greatest artistic masterpieces have been the creation of Sufis, especially in the domains of music and poetry. Sufism has also been instrumental in the central manner in the social life of Islam. Not only has Sufism revived Islamic ethics over the centuries, but the *ṭuruq* have made a direct contribution to the economic life of the community through their relation with the various guilds *(aṣnāf* and *futuwwāt)*. Sufism has also played a considerable political role, and from time to time Sufi orders have established whole dynasties, as in the case of the Ṣafavids in Persia and the Idrīsids in Libya. Finally, it is important to recall that the spread of Islam outside of the Arab and Persian worlds up to the present day has been mostly through Sufism.

Islām, Īmān, Iḥsān

To understand the hierarchical structure of the Islamic tradition better, we turn to the terms *islām, īmān,* and *iḥsān,* all of which are used in the text of the Quran and the *Ḥadīth*. The first means "surrender," the second, "faith," and the third, "virtue" or "beauty." All those who accept the Quranic revelation and surrender themselves to God are *muslim*; that is, they possess *islām*. Those who with intense faith in God and the hereafter are often referred to in the Quran as *mu'min*, that is, persons possessing faith, or *īmān*. Not every *muslim* is *mu'min*, and to this day in the Islamic world this distinction is kept clearly in mind. Those whom the Quran calls *muḥsin* are those who possess *iḥsān,* which, as mentioned already, implies a high level of spiritual perfection, the attainment of which allows human beings to live constantly with the awareness of being in God's presence; *iḥsān* is none other than that spiritual teaching that has been preserved, transmitted, and promulgated in Sufism.

A famous *ḥadīth* known as the *ḥadīth* of Gabriel gives a definition of all these terms. The *ḥadīth*, as transmitted by 'Umar, is as follows:

> *One day when we were sitting with the Messenger of God there came unto us a man whose clothes were of exceeding whiteness and whose hair was of exceeding blackness; nor were there any signs of travel upon him, although none of us knew him. He sat down knee unto knee opposite the Prophet, upon whose thighs he placed the palms of his hands saying: "O Muḥammad, tell me what is the surrender* (islām)." *The Messenger of God answered him saying: "The surrender is to testify that there is no god but God and that Muḥammad is God's Messenger, to perform the prayer, bestow the alms, fast Ramaḍān and make, if thou canst, the pilgrimage to the Holy House." He said: "Thou hast spoken truly," and we were amazed that, having questioned him, he should corroborate him. Then he said: "Tell me what is faith* (īmān)." *He answered: "To believe in God and His Angels and His Books and His Messengers and the Last Day, and to believe that no good or evil cometh but by His Providence." "Thou hast spoken truly," he said, and then: "Tell me what is excellence* (iḥsān)." *He answered: "To worship God as if thou sawest Him, for if thou seest Him not, yet seeth He thee." "Thou*

hast spoken truly," he said, and then: "Tell me of the Hour." He answered: "The questioned thereof knoweth no better than the questioner." He said: "Then tell me of its signs." He answered: "That the slave-girl shall give birth to her mistress; and that those who were but barefoot naked needy herdsmen shall build buildings ever higher and higher." Then the stranger went away, and I stayed a while after he had gone; and the Prophet said to me: "O 'Umar, knowest thou the questioner, who he was?" I said: "God and His Messenger know best." He said: "It was Gabriel. He came unto you to teach you your religion."[9]

When one thinks of the term "Islam" as used in the English language to denote the whole tradition, one must think not only of *islām,* but also of *īmān* and *iḥsān.* The teachings of Islam have levels of meaning, and the religion consists of a hierarchy that, destined to become the religion of a large portion of humanity, had to accommodate the spiritual and intellectual needs of the simplest peasant and the most astute philosopher, the warrior and the lover, the jurist and the mystic. Islam achieved this goal by making the teachings of religion accessible on various levels from the most outward to the most inward. But it preserved unity by insisting that all of the members of its community share in the Sacred Law and the central doctrine of *al-tawḥīd* summarized in "*Lā ilāha illa'Llāh.*" Their degree of penetration into the meaning of Unity depended and continues to depend on the intensity of their faith and the beauty of their soul. But in submission to the One *(al-islām)*, all Muslims stand in the same manner before God in a single community governed by the bonds of brotherhood and sisterhood as well as amity. Paradoxically, the multiple inner dimensions of the religion do not destroy this unity, but in fact only strengthen it, because these inner and higher modes of participation in the religion bring worshipers ever closer to the One. Unity is thereby strengthened, even in the more outward aspects of human life that all Muslims share, whatever their degree of participation might be in the understanding and practice of Islam.

5

Islamic Practices, Ethics, and Institutions

The Pillars: Prayer, Fasting, Pilgrimage, and Almsgiving

The basic rites of Islam revealed to the Prophet and institutionalized by him are usually called the *arkān*, or "pillars," of the religion, for on them rests the whole ritual structure of the religion. These rites include the canonical prayers (*ṣalāh* in Arabic and *namāz* in Persian), fasting (*ṣawm* in Arabic and *rūzah* in Persian), pilgrimage (*ḥajj*), and the paying of a tithe or religious tax (*zakāh*). To these *arkān* is usually added the important act of *jihād*, which, as already mentioned, is usually mistranslated into English as "holy war," but literally means "exertion" or "effort" in the path of God. This act must be seen, however, not as another pillar, but as an element that must be present in the whole of life, especially in the performance of the rites and acts of worship.

The canonical prayers—*ṣalāh*—are the most central rite of Islam. They are incumbent on all Muslims, both male and female, from the age of adolescence until death. They punctuate the Muslim's daily life and place him or her directly, without any intermediary, before God. The prayers must be performed in the direction of the Ka'bah in Mecca five times a day: in the early morning, between dawn and sunrise; at noon; in the afternoon; at sunset; and at night before midnight. They are preceded by the call to prayer *(adhān)* and ritual ablution *(wuḍū')* and can be performed on any ritually clean ground whether outdoors or indoors as long as one has the permission of the owner. The units *(rak'ah)* of prayer differ on each occasion: two in the morning, four at noon, four in the afternoon, three in the evening, and four at night. All the movements, postures, and words follow the model established by the Prophet. In the *ṣalāh,* men and women pray to God in the name of the whole of creation and as God's vicegerents on earth. The *ṣalāh* makes possible the integration of the worshiper's whole being in the state of perfect servitude to God. For people of *īmān* and *iḥsān,* it is the very means of ascent to the Throne of God according to the saying: "The *ṣalāh* is the spiritual ascent of the faithful" *(al-ṣalāh mi'rāj al-mu'min).* The ascent refers to the Nocturnal Ascent, or *mi'rāj,* of the Prophet.

The daily *ṣalāh* is often performed at home or in the fields but can be and is, of course, also often performed in mosques (the term "mosque" is derived from the Arabic word *masjid,* meaning "the place of prostration," which is the penultimate movement in the *ṣalāh* and designates total submission to

God). In addition to the *ṣalāh,* there are the Friday congregational prayers, which are almost always performed in mosques or in their absence in open spaces in towns, in the fields, or in the desert. They bring the members of the community together and have important social, economic, and even political dimensions as well as a purely religious one. During these prayers a sermon is delivered by the leader of the prayers *(imām).* Throughout Islamic history, mention of the name of the ruler in such sermons has had a great deal to do with the legitimacy of his rule. Most of the sermon is, however, usually spent on ethical and moral issues, and after the prayers money is usually given to the poor. There are also special canonical prayers associated with the end of Ramaḍān and the end of the rite of pilgrimage. *Ṣalāh* is also offered at times of great fear or need to beseech God for help and at times of joy to offer thanksgiving.

In addition to the *ṣalāh,* individual prayers *(du'ā)* are performed after the *ṣalāh* or at other times during the day and night. Some of these *du'ās* are more formal because they are set prayers formulated by great saints and religious authorities of old. Others are simply individual, personal prayers recited in one's own mother tongue. The *ṣalāh,* however, is always performed in Arabic, for it is a rite whose form is sacred and beyond the individual, a Divine norm in which men and women take refuge from the withering effects of the storm of life and the transient conditions of temporal existence.

The obligatory fast in Islam—*ṣawm*—consists of complete abstention from all food and drink from the first moment of dawn to sunset (or dusk in Shīʿism) during the holy month of Ramaḍān. It also requires abstention from all sexual activity and all illicit acts as designated by the *Sharīʿah*. Moreover, the fast requires keeping one's mind and tongue away from evil thoughts and words and being especially considerate to the destitute. The fast is required of all Muslims, male and female, from the age of adolescence until one no longer possesses the physical strength to undertake it. The sick and those on a journey are not required to fast, but they must try to make up the days lost when possible. Also, women do not fast, just as they do not perform the *ṣalāh*, during their menstrual period; breast-feeding mothers also do not fast. The month of Ramaḍān is when the Quran first descended on the soul of the Prophet, during the night called the "Night of Power" *(laylat al-qadr)*. It is therefore a very blessed month during which much time is given to prayer and the recitation of the Quran. The month ends with the greatest Muslim religious holiday, the *ʿīd al-fiṭr*, which is celebrated for several days in most countries. The formal end of the month of fasting comes with the congregational prayers of the *ʿīd*, after which a sum of money equal to the cost of all the meals not eaten by oneself and one's family during the month is usually given to the poor.

Ḥajj is the supreme pilgrimage of Islam and is made to the Kaʿbah, or House of God, in Mecca. This rite, instituted by Abraham and revived by the Prophet of Islam, involves circumambulation around the Kaʿbah, certain movements, prayers, and the sacrifice of an animal in Mecca and adjoining areas according to the norms established by the Prophet. The *ḥajj* signifies a return both to the spatial center of the Islamic universe and to the temporal origin of the human state itself. Muslims believe that God forgives a person's sins if he or she performs the *ḥajj* with devotion and sincerity. The *ḥajj* is performed during the Islamic lunar month of Dhu'l-ḥijjah and is obligatory for all men and women who have the financial and physical means to accomplish it. During the past few years, over 2 million annual pilgrims from the Philippines to Morocco and Russia to South Africa, including American and European Muslims, have made the *ḥajj* into a rite unique in its grandeur, size, and diversity.

In addition to the great pilgrimage, it is also possible to make the lesser *ḥajj*, or *ḥajj al-'umrah*, to Mecca at any time during the year. Muslims also make pilgrimage to Medina and, when they could, to Jerusalem. There are also many local sites of pilgrimage in most Muslim lands—for example, the two Moulay Idrīses in Fez and near Meknes, Ra's al-Ḥusayn in Cairo, the site of the remains of Imām Ḥusayn in Karbalā', the tombs of Imām 'Alī in Najaf, Imām Riḍā in Mashhad, Dādā Ganjbakhsh in Lahore, and Shaykh Mu'īn al-Dīn Chishtī in Ajmer—all of which attract hundreds of thousands of pilgrims every year. To this day pilgrimage remains a major part of the religious and devotional life of Muslims.

The term *zakāh* in Arabic is related to the word for "purity." *Zakāh* is the religious tax stipulated by the *Sharī'ah* to be paid by all Muslims who have enough income to do so to purify their wealth and make it legitimate *(ḥalāl)* in the eyes of God.

The tax collected in this way is to be kept in the "public treasury" *(bayt al-māl)* and spent for public and religious services and works, including supporting needy students and feeding the poor. In addition, other religious taxes have been devised to bring about a more just distribution of wealth and prevent hoarding and excessive amassing of wealth by one individual or group.

The Meaning of Exertion in the Path of God: Jihād

In the West, Islam is often associated with holy war, despite the fact that the Crusades were ordered by the Cluny monks and the pope, not a Muslim ruler or religious authority. This deeply ingrained distortion of the image of Islam going back to these and other events has caused the Arabic term *jihād* to be translated as "holy war," but it means simply "exertion in the path of God." Recent constant reference to this term by both extremist Muslims and Western media has caused its authentic meaning to become totally eclipsed. Of course, one meaning of *jihād* is to struggle to protect Islam and its borders, but the term has much a wider usage and meaning for Muslims.

First, every religious act, such as performing the *ṣalāh* regularly day in and day out for a whole lifetime or fasting for fourteen hours in a hot climate, requires *jihād*; in fact, the whole of life may be said to be a constant *jihād* between our carnal and passionate soul and the demands of the immortal spirit within us. It was in reference to this profounder meaning of *jihād* that the Prophet said to his companions after a major battle in which the very existence of the early Islamic community was at stake, "Verily ye have returned from the lesser *jihād* to the greater *jihād*." And when one of the companions asked what the greater *jihād* was, he answered, "to battle against your passionate souls *(nafs)*." Islam, therefore, sees *jihād* as vigilance against all that distracts us from God and exertion to do His Will within ourselves as well as preserving and reestablishing the order and harmony that He has willed for Islamic society and the world about us.

Specifically Shī'ite Practices

In addition to all the rites mentioned above, which are performed by all Muslims, Shī'ites perform certain other rites and practices. To this day, Shī'ites mourn the martyrdom of the grandson of the Prophet, Ḥusayn ibn 'Alī, in Karbalā' in Iraq by the army of Yazīd, the Umayyad caliph. This event, which took place during the month of Muḥarram in the year 61/680, is remembered for fifty days beginning with the first day of that month, which also marks the commencement of the Islamic lunar year, and culminating in the tenth day, marking the date of Imām Ḥusayn's death. During Muḥarram there are vast religious processions, in which mourners sometimes beat their chests *(sīnah-zanī)*; gatherings in which the tragedy of Karbalā' is recounted *(rawḍah-khānī)*; and passion plays *(ta'ziyah)*, which represent the only religious theater of consequence in the Islamic world. Some of these events in Iran, Iraq, Lebanon, Pakistan, and India reach monumental dimensions and are among the most moving religious events in the Islamic world.

Shīʿites also emphasize the importance of pilgrimage to the tombs of the Imāms in addition to pilgrimage to Mecca, Medina, and Jerusalem. Pilgrimage to such places as Najaf, where the tomb of ʿAlī is located; Karbalāʾ, the site of the tomb of his son Ḥusayn; Kāẓimayn, of the seventh and ninth Imāms; Samarrah, of the tenth and eleventh Imāms; and Mashhad, of the eighth Imām—as well as to the tombs of the descendants of the Imāms such as the mausoleum of Qum, where the sister of Imām Riḍā is buried—are among the most notable features of Shīʿite religious life. Shīʿites recite many liṭanies and prayers inherited from the Imāms, especially during Ramaḍān and Muḥarram, in addition to the regular recitation of the Quran.

Islamic Ethics

The whole life of Muslims is permeated by ethical consideration, as Islam does not accept the legitimacy of any domain —whether social, political, or economic—falling outside of ethical consideration. The principles of all Islamic ethics are to be found in the Quran and *Ḥadīth*, which exhort Muslims to perform what is good and to refrain from what is evil. The ultimate criterion of what constitutes good and evil resides in revelation, although over the centuries an important debate has gone on between various schools of Islamic theology concerning the role of intelligence, as a God-given gift to human beings, in distinguishing between good and evil. Some have asserted that God has given human beings *al-'aql* (which means both "intellect" and "reason"), with which they can discern good from evil precisely because this gift is given by God, who is the source of all goodness. Others have insisted that whatever God has willed as good is good and as evil is evil and that the *'aql* has no power to make such a distinction by itself. Whatever the theological position, however, Islam has avoided the kind of humanistic ethics that claim to know good and evil and to guide human beings to act ethically independently of God. Even the rational ethics of Islamic philosophers are grounded in the reality that the good comes from God and has an ontological reality related to the Divine Nature.

There are many theological and philosophical treatments of ethics, especially the question of good and evil, in Islamic thought. Few major questions in this area treated by Western thinkers over the centuries have not been dealt with amply in Islamic sources. Islamic thought, however, never accepted the divorce between ethics and religion, which was one of the results of the development of postmedieval humanism in the West. Nor has the question of theodicy, that is, the problem of God, who is good, creating a world in which there is evil, ever led Islamic philosophers to that flight from the world of faith that one has seen in the West during the past five centuries.

It is important to emphasize ethics as lived and practiced in Islamic society in addition to the theological and philosophical dimensions of the issue. On the practical level, ethics are intertwined with the *Sharīʿah,* which, as Divine Law, weds all legal matters to ethical concerns. Whether it is a question of work ethics, social ethics in general, or the ethics of individual behavior, the *Sharīʿah* remains the guide for Muslim behavior. Also, throughout Islamic history, Sufis have sought to interiorize the ethical teachings of the *Sharīʿah* and breathe new spirit into Islamic ethics and ethical behavior by living virtuously in the highest sense of this term and guiding others toward living according to ethical norms seen in their inward dimension. The most influential works of Islamic ethics over the centuries have, in fact, been treatises written by Sufis, of which the most important, as far as the extent of its impact is concerned, is the *Iḥyāʾ ʿulūm al-dīn* ("The Revivification of the Sciences of Religion") by Abū Ḥāmid Muḥammad al-Ghazzālī, the great Sufi and theologian of the fifth/eleventh century, who wrote this monumental work in Arabic and then summarized it himself in Persian in his *Kīmiyā-yi saʿādat* ("Alchemy of Happiness"). One might say that the goal of Islam is, on the one hand, the creation of a moral order in human society and, on the other, spiritual realization based on the inculcation of the spiritual virtues within the inner being of men and women.

The Family

The society envisaged by Islam and dominated by Islamic ethical norms is an organic whole in which various institutions and units are intertwined. Of these institutions, which range from the state to the most local social unit, none is more important than the family, whose bonds are greatly emphasized in Islam. The Quran exhorts Muslims to respect their parents, and many *ḥadīths* emphasize how pleasing it is in the eyes of God to preserve the bonds of family and especially to respect and honor one's mother and father. The strength of the family in Islamic society is so great that it alone, among all the major social institutions of Islam, has remained practically intact even through the major dislocations that much of the Islamic world has undergone during the past two centuries.

The Muslim family does not consist only of parents and children, as one observes in the atomized family of modern urban society in the West. Rather, the Muslim family is still, for the most part, the extended family, consisting of grandparents, uncles and aunts, cousins, and in-laws as well as parents and children. The father is like the imām of the family, representing religious authority. He is responsible for both the economic welfare of the members of the family and the preservation of the teachings of religion among them. But the actual religious instruction often depends on the mother, especially in the earlier stages, and Muslim women play a dominant role in every other aspect of home life as well as in the education of the children.

Although usually the Muslim male dominates in economic and social activity outside the home, it is the wife who reigns completely in the home, where the husband is like a guest. It is the wife who is central to family life and who provides most of the social bonding among members of the family. Women exert a much greater influence through the family within the whole of society than an outward study of what appears to be a patriarchal religious structure would indicate. The most important concrete reality in the life of a Muslim after God, the Prophet, and the spiritual and religious figures, who are in a sense an extension of the Prophet, is the family; the most important figures who preserve the organic bonds within the family are the women, who as wives, mothers, sisters, and mothers-in-law usually wield great power and influence over the whole family.

All family relations, whether they are between husband and wife, parents and children, or other members of the family, are governed by religious injunctions. The family is seen by Muslims not only as a biological and social unit, but also as a religious unit that protects the individual member in a thousand ways. This unit nurtures and trains individuals, forms the immediate social reality in which the first lessons of religion are taught, and is the "world" in which religious injunctions must be constantly applied and practiced. Muslims live between two powerful social realities: the *ummah,* or the whole of the Islamic community, whose total reality they cannot grasp but with which they ideally identify, and the family, which for individual Muslims constitutes the most real part of their world. All other institutions, whether they are economic or political, occupy a secondary rank in comparison with them. And between the two, the family remains the most immediately palpable and therefore constitutes the most basic unit in the fabric of Islamic society.

Nomadic and Sedentary Life

While emphasizing family bonds within the context of Islam, from the beginning the teachings of Islam sought to combat the tribal bonds that were so strong in the world into which Islam was born. Throughout its history, Islamic civilization has been witness to the confrontation and complementarity between nomadic life based on tribal structures and sedentary life. The Arabia of the Prophet was dominated by various tribes, and allegiance to the tribe was of paramount importance in the life of the Arabs. Islam sought to break this tribal bond in favor of the bond that unites all Muslims in one *ummah.* Despite great success, which did create a single Islamic people, however, tribal bonds continued to persist to some extent, especially among those who preserved the nomadic way of life. They have not totally died out by any means, even today when so many nomads have been forced to settle in towns.

Besides the Arabs, the Turks and Mongols who invaded the eastern lands of Islam were also nomads, and in many countries from Afghanistan and Persia to Morocco and Mauritania there existed over the centuries and continues to exist to some extent today an interplay of the greatest significance between nomadic and sedentary life. Nomads gave to the sedentary centers a new blood, simplicity of life and mores, discipline, and religious intensity and fervor. The sedentary population provided finesse and cultivation of knowledge and the arts, but its culture also led to excessive luxury and moral decadence, which needed periodic rejuvenation by the nomadic element. A rhythm was thereby created between the two major constitutive elements of Islamic society, a rhythm the understanding of which is basic to a better grasp of the dynamics of Islamic civilization. It was the great Tunisian historian Ibn Khaldūn who, in the eighth/fourteenth century, analyzed this rhythm so masterfully in his *Muqaddimah* ("Prolegomena") and who revealed its significance as well as that of the power of the forces that held tribes and various ethnic units together over the centuries. To this day tribal bonds inherited from the nomadic life of earlier periods remain of much significance in many parts of Islamic society and intertwine, in many cases, with the bonds and structures of the extended family, to which they are obviously related. Yet the traditional relation between nomads and sedentary people is now for the most part broken and the rhythm described by Ibn Khaldūn no longer exists.

Economic Activity and the Craft Guilds

Economics as a distinct discipline is a modern invention, but economic activity has, of course, been an integral part of every human culture. Islam, therefore, sought to integrate all that would be called economics today into its unitary and religious perspective. Many Quranic injunctions and *ḥadīths* bear directly on economic life, such as the ban on usury *(ribā')*, which is considered strictly forbidden *(ḥarām)* by Islamic Law, and the excessive amassing of wealth in private hands. Islam also consigns many forms of wealth, such as forests and certain types of water resources, to the public sector, while emphasizing the right of private property as long as the appropriate religious and legal conditions are fulfilled. In reality, from the Islamic point of view, all possessions belong ultimately to God, but God has given the right of private property to human beings as long as they remain aware that it is a trust from Him. They must therefore pay the required religious taxes, follow licit means of gaining wealth, and help the poor to the extent that they can. There is a strong relation between economic activity and religious ethics in traditional Islamic society and throughout Islamic history, and up to now, there has always been a close link between the class of merchants and the religious scholars (*'ulamā'*). To this day the bazaars of Islamic cities, that is, the locus of traditional economic activity, have also remained centers of intense religious activity, and traditional merchants are among the most pious members of Islamic society. One could say that in the Islamic perspective economics can never be divorced from ethics and that the former independent of the latter is, religiously speaking, illegitimate.

One of the most important economic institutions through which religious values and attitudes have been propagated in Islamic society is the guilds (*aṣnāf* or *futuwwāt*), some of which still survive in parts of the Islamic world. *Futuwwah* (*jawānmardī* in Persian), which can be rendered as "spiritual chivalry," was originally more closely connected with the military class than with the craft guilds and merchants. Toward the end of the 'Abbāsid caliphate in the seventh/thirteenth century, it became more associated with the crafts and has remained so during the past eight centuries. *Futuwwah*—which means the combination of the virtues of courage, nobility, and selflessness—was associated from the beginning of Islamic history with the name of 'Alī, who is considered the master of *futuwwah* and in a sense the "patron saint" of the guilds. Some guilds, however, are considered by their members to have been founded at the beginning of human history by the son of Adam, Seth. The qualities associated with *futuwwah* gradually became incorporated into the guilds, which were often linked to Sufi orders and in which the art of making and producing objects from cloth to buildings was combined with religious and spiritual considerations.

The guilds are usually headed by a master *(ustādh),* who not only teaches the disciple the techniques of the art or craft in question, but also inculcates moral and spiritual discipline in the student. The process of the production of objects, which then enter the marketplace, is thus combined with religious and spiritual training. The profoundly religious character of traditional Islamic art, from the central sacred arts of calligraphy and architecture to the art of creating objects for everyday use such as carpets, textiles, or utensils for the home, is related to the structure and nature of the guilds, which over the centuries have produced most of the objects of Islamic art. In Islam, art is not considered a luxury, but an integral part of life itself, and everything has its special art *(fann)* by virtue of which it can be made or done correctly. Through the guilds, Islam was able to imbue its arts and crafts, which are inseparable from the arts, with the deepest values of the Islamic religion and thereby to Islamize completely the atmosphere in which the traditional Muslim lived and functioned. Without doubt, the guilds are among the most important of Islamic economic institutions, responsible for linking the production of objects to the deepest ethos of Islam. If Islamic art reflects what lies at the heart of the Islamic message, it is because this art issues from the inner dimension of the Islamic tradition and is executed and produced, thanks to the guilds, by those for whom the process and technique of making things has remained inseparable from the supreme art, which is the perfecting of the soul and drawing it nigh unto God—a goal that constitutes the heart of the Islamic message.

Religious Endowments

Another major Islamic institution that plays an important economic and social role is that of *waqf,* or religious endowment. The Arabic term means literally "arresting" or "taking into custody" a sum of money or assets. The person or persons designated by the endower receive the money or assets, and the person contributing them determines their purpose and the manner of their administration. Any purpose that is in accordance with the *Sharīʿah* and is not illicit can be chosen, ranging from establishing schools to building water fountains. Throughout Islamic history wealthy patrons have created *waqfs* with either monetary assets, land, or other forms of wealth. These *waqfs* have created and maintained mosques, schools, Sufi centers, hospitals for both people and animals, homes for the elderly, sanatoriums, roads and bridges, wells and water fountains, hospices for pilgrims, and many other public works.

The most important function of *waqf,* however, after the purely religious one associated with the construction and maintenance of mosques and similar buildings, has probably been educational. In Islamic civilization before the advent of modernism, education was always in private hands and not a governmental responsibility. Nor is there a church in Islam, as one finds in Christianity, that could direct educational activity. Throughout the Islamic world, various educational institutions, from the simple Quranic schools in mosques to the *madrasahs,* which are the model for medieval Western universities, were sustained until modern times mostly by private contributions, income from religious taxes, and *waqfs* and continue to be supported in this manner to this day, although government-run educational institutions now complement and in many places have replaced the traditional schools.

In traditional Islamic civilization, even when schools were established by governmental authorities such as kings or ministers, these acts were performed by them qua individuals and not as agents of the government. The best example is the famous university system called the Niẓāmiyyah, founded by the Persian prime minister of the Seljūqs, Khwājah Niẓām al-Mulk, in the fifth/eleventh century, with centers in Baghdad, Nayshapur, and elsewhere. The whole system was supported by a *waqf* established by Khwājah Niẓām al-Mulk as a private individual, not in his function as prime minister. In modern times, in most Islamic countries, the institution of *waqf,* along with the immense assets that the *waqfs* possess in each country, have been taken over by governments and administered by ministries usually bearing the name of *awqāf* (plural of *waqf*). But even under such conditions, the *waqf* remains an important religious institution for furthering religious and charitable causes within society, and wealthy Muslims continue to establish new *waqfs* along the lines that have been followed throughout Islamic history.

Political Institutions

Islam has never separated religion from politics the way the Gospels mention dividing the kingdoms of God and Caesar. The Prophet himself was both the religious and the political leader of the first Islamic community established in Medina, and since the advent of that ideal Islamic society, every period of Islamic history has witnessed the interplay between religion (as the term is currently understood) and politics. And yet neither the Quran nor the *Ḥadīth* provides clear instructions as to what political institutions or models should be established. What they do establish is the principle that God is the ultimate ruler of the Islamic community; from Him descends all power and legitimacy, and His Law should be the law of every Islamic society. Another central principle is that rulers must consult *(shawrā)* with the people in matters pertaining to political rule. One should therefore say, strictly speaking, that Islam believes in nomocracy, that is, the rule of Divine Law, rather than theocracy, which is usually understood as the rule of the priesthood or the church.

After the death of the Prophet, the caliphate (from the Arabic *khilāfah*), the most important of all Islamic political institutions, developed and survived in one form or another until the seventh/thirteenth century, despite the opposition of various Shī'ite groups and other elements. The caliph was considered the vicegerent *(khalīfah)* of the Prophet; as such, his function was to promulgate the Divine Law, preserve internal order, protect the borders of *dār al-islām*, and appoint judges to officiate in *Sharī'ite* courts. The caliph was not expected to possess knowledge of the inner meaning of the Divine Law or even be an authority (in the sense of *faqīh* or *mujtahid*) in the Law. Shī'ites disagreed on this last point and opposed the selection of the caliph by consensus, insisting that he had to be appointed by the previous legitimate ruler (for them, the Imām), hence keeping intact the line of succession going back to the Prophet, and also confirmed by Divine decree.

Gradually the actual military power of the caliphs diminished; real military and political power fell into the hands of local kings, and the caliph retained only nominal authority. Under these conditions, a new religious theory of political authority was developed by the Sunni jurists *(fuqahā')*, in which the caliph remained the symbol of the unity of the Islamic community and the rule of the *Sharī'ah*, and the king or *sulṭān*, with actual military and political power, had the duty to preserve public order and protect the borders of the Islamic world. This theory, which received its best-known formulations in the work of such famous religious authorities as al-Māwardī and al-Ghazzālī in the fifth/eleventh century, was held by some into the twentieth century, until the downfall of the Ottoman caliphate (which many considered to be a sultanate and not a real caliphate), and still survives among many Sunni Muslims. Historically, the Shīʿites rejected the institution of the Sunni caliphate. The Twelve-Imām Shīʿites, who expect the coming of the Mahdī, accepted in his absence the monarchy as the most suitable form of government in the imperfect conditions of the world deprived of the direct presence of the Imām. With the Iranian Revolution of 1979, this traditional view was challenged and rejected by Ayatollah Khomeini, who substituted for it the theory of the "vicarage of the jurisprudent" *(wilāyat-i faqīh)*.

It is important to understand the role of the traditional *ʿulamāʾ*, or religious scholars, in various Islamic political theories as well as in practice. As interpreters and guardians of the *Sharīʿah*, the *ʿulamāʾ* have always wielded political power in the Islamic world, although they never ruled directly anywhere until the Iranian Revolution of 1979. In this context it needs also to be emphasized that the Shīʿite *ʿulamāʾ* have usually been more tightly organized and politically and economically more powerful than their Sunni counterparts.

The relation between Islam and political life is a very complex one. Throughout its history, Islam created political institutions such as the caliphate and sultanate, which came to be challenged with the advent of modernism and the colonial domination of much of the Islamic world by a West in which the traditional ideas of political rule had been seriously challenged by several revolutions. Among these, the French Revolution had the greatest impact on the Islamic world. The result of the weakening or destruction of traditional Islamic political institutions is seen in the political turmoil that has encompassed much of the Islamic world in recent times. But whatever the crises and the forces involved in a particular situation, the nexus between Islam and political life endures and has not been severed. If Muslims were to accept in principle the separation of religion from the domain of public life (which would then become secularized, as it has in the West to an ever greater degree since the Renaissance), they would have to abandon the doctrine of Unity that lies at the heart of the Islamic message. They would have to act against the *Sunnah* of the Prophet and fourteen centuries of the historical unfolding of the Islamic tradition. It remains, however, for contemporary Islamic society to develop political institutions that are authentically Islamic and respond at the same time to the challenges of the day.

6

A Brief Journey Through Islamic History

The Age of the Prophet and the Four Rightly Guided Caliphs

The history of Islam is inseparable from the history of Islamic society, institutions, and civilization in which the transhistorical realities of Islam have been manifested, although of course those realities are not themselves of purely historical origin. Moreover, Islamic history provides a temporal cadre within which one can situate the history of the religion itself, even if the ebbs and flows and beginnings and ends of various modes and schools of Islamic thought are not always identical with the periods of Islamic history marked by dynastic and political changes.

The period from the migration of the Prophet, which marks the establishment of the first Islamic society in Medina, to his death and the caliphate of the first four caliphs (i.e., from

1/622 to 40/661) constitutes a unique period in Islamic history. It is to some extent similar to the apostolic age in Christianity, and it is an era to which Muslims have looked for guidance throughout their later history. The earthly career of the Prophet, already discussed, was followed by the caliphate of Abū Bakr from 11/632 to 13/634. He was the first of the four caliphs accepted by Sunni Muslims as the rightly guided caliphs *(al-khulafā' al-rāshidūn)* and considered to be men of great sanctity and piety, whose political rule was marked by profound religious considerations even if they might have committed occasional errors of political judgment. Abū Bakr, who ruled for only two years, was faced almost immediately with the centrifugal forces of Arab tribalism, which threatened to break up the political unity of Arabia created by the Prophet. Abū Bakr's greatest contribution was to put down tribal uprisings and to preserve the unity of the newly founded political entity with its capital in Medina.

The second caliph, 'Umar, who ruled from 13/634 to 23/644, followed Abū Bakr's lead and insisted on a strong center that could preserve the unity of the Islamic state, which was beginning to expand. It was during his rule that Muslims captured Jerusalem, where 'Umar showed great respect for the houses of worship of Jews and Christians, and Islam spread into Syria, Persia, and North Africa. 'Umar lived a life of remarkable simplicity and austerity and, like Abū Bakr, was a paragon of piety. Most Sunnis consider 'Umar's rule the most successful, from a practical point of view, among all the rightly guided caliphs, a rule that witnessed the establishment of many administrative practices and institutions that became permanent features of later Islamic society.

'Umar was succeeded by 'Uthmān, who was chosen, like all the *rāshidūn,* by consensus of the elders of the community. His rule, from 23/644 to 35/656, saw the influx of wealth into Medina and the rest of Arabia from conquests in the provinces, although tensions resulted, including tribal uprisings. Many also criticized 'Uthmān for the practice of nepotism, especially in appointing his relative Mu'āwiyah to the governorship of Syria. The opposition to 'Uthmān finally caused an uprising against him led by the son of Abū Bakr, which resulted in 'Uthmān's death, an event of grave consequence for later Islamic history, for it was to avenge the death of his uncle 'Uthmān that Mu'āwiyah moved against 'Uthmān's successor, 'Alī, and precipitated the division in the body politic that has persisted to this day.

'Alī, who ruled from 35/656 to 40/661, was faced almost immediately with civil strife and even war on many fronts. His followers *(shī'ah)* battled some of the Quraysh, on one hand, and the Prophet's companions Talḥah and Zubayr, who were joined by the Prophet's wife 'Ā'ishah, on the other, and were victorious against both. With the majority of his supporters in Iraq, 'Alī moved the capital of Islam to Kufa and from there set out to confront the Syrian garrisons of Mu'āwiyah, who had refused to pay allegiance to 'Alī. The two sides fought the crucial battle of Ṣiffīn in 36/657, in which 'Alī was victorious, but at the moment of victory Mu'āwiyah had his army come to the battlefield with Qurans on their lances, asking that the Quran arbitrate between the two sides. To avoid desecration of the sacred book, 'Alī accepted arbitration in which his side lost to the much more astute representatives of Mu'āwiyah. 'Alī returned to Kufa, where, in 40/661, a member of a group that opposed arbitration in principle and considered both sides in the battle to have deviated from the earlier norms of Islam killed 'Alī and brought to an end the rule of the *rāshidūn*. One can say that from the time of the battle of Ṣiffīn, the distinction between the Sunnis, the Shī'ites, and a third group called the Khārijites (literally, those who "stand outside,"opposed to both Sunnism and Shī'ism) became marked, only to be accentuated by later events, especially the martyrdom of 'Alī's son Ḥusayn in Karbalā'. Also, 'Alī's transfer of the capital to Kufa moved the political and cultural center of the Islamic world permanently outside Arabia, although the religious center remained and continues to remain in the Hejaz.

The Classical Caliphates: Umayyad and 'Abbāsid

THE UMAYYADS (40/661-132/750)

With 'Alī removed from the scene, Mu'āwiyah became the ruler and caliph of the Islamic world, although for a few months 'Alī's son al-Ḥasan continued to claim the caliphate in Medina. Mu'āwiyah, who was a very competent and calculating ruler, was able to establish a vast empire with Damascus as its center, but at the cost of converting the caliphate of the *rāshidūn* to a hereditary sultanate. The Umayyads were able to rule from Central Asia to Spain and France, establishing a system of communication, administration, and legal and military institutions, much of which survived over the centuries. They were faced with attempts to restore the power of the aristocracy of Mecca and bedouin rebellion against central authority, as well as Shī'ite dissent. 'Abd al-Malik (65/685-86/705) succeeded in securing the unity of the empire, but, increasingly, the pious saw religious principles sacrificed before worldly ends, although one of the caliphs, 'Umar ibn 'Abd al-'Azīz, who sought to reform the existing economic system, was a model of piety and highly revered not only by the Sunni faithful, but even by Shī'ites, whom he treated with kindness.

The Umayyads strengthened the administrative and military foundations of the empire and Arabized coinage and the chancelleries. They completed the early conquests and permitted Islamic culture to establish itself from the Oxus to the Pyrenees. And yet they began to lose the support of many Muslims and therefore their "legitimacy." Many considered them to be Arab rather than Islamic rulers, and resentment grew against them, especially among *mawālī,* that is, non-Arabs, who had embraced Islam in ever greater numbers, chief among whom were the Persians. Much of this protest took place under the banner of Shī'ism and centered in Iraq, especially after the death of Ḥusayn ibn 'Alī during the caliphate of Yazīd. The opposition, however, was kept at bay by strong governors, but it gradually spread farther east until in Khurasan, under the leadership of the charismatic Persian general Abū Muslim, an uprising began with the purpose of returning the caliphate to its religious origin and the family of the Prophet. The movement succeeded, and the Banū 'Abbās, descendants of the uncle of the Prophet, defeated the Umayyads and captured Damascus with the help of their Persian supporters, bringing the rule of the Umayyads to an end. The only exception was Muslim Spain, where one of the Umayyads who had been able to flee from Damascus established himself as ruler and inaugurated the golden age of Muslim rule in that land.

THE 'ABBĀSIDS (132/750-656/1258)

'Abbāsid rule marks the period in which what is usually called "classical Islamic civilization" reached its apogee. The early 'Abbāsids continued the work of the Umayyads in strengthening the Islamic empire, preserving its unity, Islamizing various institutions, and spreading further the use of Arabic as the lingua franca of the empire. It was also during their rule that Persian developed and became the second lingua franca of the Islamic world. While reasserting the sacred character of the caliphate, the 'Abbāsids began to emulate Persian models of rule and administration to an ever greater degree. The capital was moved eastward toward Persia when al-Manṣūr built Baghdad in 145/762 near the ancient Sassanid capital of Ctesiphon, near the heartland of the Persian world. Persians also became much more active in affairs of state, and many of them served as chief ministers to the caliphs.

Baghdad soon became the greatest cultural center of the Islamic world, perhaps of the whole of the world, in the third/ninth and fourth/tenth centuries. Famous 'Abbāsid caliphs such as Hārūn al-Rashīd and al-Ma'mūn were great patrons of the arts and sciences, and it was at this time that both Islamic philosophy and science began to flourish. But the early 'Abbāsid period was also the era when the codification of *Sharī'ite* Law, begun during the Umayyad period, was finalized and the traditional schools of Law as they subsist to this day were established. Almost certainly the most important religious achievement of this period was the establishment of the definitive and canonical collections of *Ḥadīth* by Bukhārī and others, an achievement that was, again, the culmination of the process begun during the time of the *rāshidūn* and continued in the Umayyad period. Likewise, the early 'Abbāsid period coincides with the rise of the classical schools of Sufism in both Baghdad and Khurasan.

Gradually, however, the power of the 'Abbāsid caliphate began to wane. Caught amid rivalries between Arabs and Persians, the caliphs sought to surround themselves with Turkic guards, thus opening the center of the Islamic world to a third major ethnic group, after the Arabs and Persians, which was to play an ever greater role in the sociopolitical life of the central regions of the caliphate. Soon the caliphs became pawns in the hands of their own Turkic generals. Caught in the tension between the agrarian population and city dwellers and between the military and civil administrations and battling problems of land and taxation and ethnic rivalries, the center finally ceased to be able to hold the vast Islamic empire together. Regional rulers gained power to the extent that the Persian Būyids captured Iraq itself in 334/945, and made the caliph their instrument of rule to legitimize the power that was in reality in their hands. Henceforth, local dynasties wielded actual political power, while the caliphate became the symbol of the unity of the Islamic world and the rule of the *Sharīʿah* as well as the source of legitimacy for various kings or sultans who governed not only in Persia, but also in many Arab lands.

Local Dynasties up to the Mongol Invasion

PERSIA, CENTRAL ASIA, AND TRANSOXIANA

As early as the third/ninth century, local governors in the eastern provinces of Persia were beginning to assert their independence from the central authority of the caliphate in Baghdad, and they soon established the first independent Persian dynasties, such as the Ṣaffārids and Sāmānids. The latter, who ruled in Khurasan and Central Asia into the fourth/tenth century, are especially important from a cultural point of view, because they were the great patrons of the Persian language, which soon became a basic factor in the cultural and political independence that the Persians were asserting vis-à-vis Arab domination. Semi-independent dynasties also began to appear in northern and western areas of Persia; one, the Būyids, conquered not only Persia, but Iraq as well during the fourth/tenth century, and ruled as Shīʿites supported by strong Persian national sentiments.

The advance of tribes of Turkic stock changed the political and even ethnic landscape of the territory governed by the Sāmānids, especially Central Asia. The Ghaznavids, who were of Turkic origin, defeated the Sāmānids and established a powerful kingdom in eastern Persia, extending their realm to Sindh and the Punjab. Their rule set the background for the appearance of a number of dynasties of Turkic stock who began to dominate the political scene not only in Central Asia and Persia, but in certain Arab lands, parts of India, and Anatolia as well.

THE SELJŪQS

The most important of the Turkic dynasties was the Seljūqs, who ruled for more than two centuries, from about 426/1035 to 656/1258. The Seljūqs conquered most of western Asia, including Baghdad itself, which fell into the hands of Tughrïl Beg in 447/1055. They reunified western Asia once again, preserving the ʿAbbāsid caliphate, but only as a symbol of Sunni rule, which they avidly supported. They opposed the power of local Shīʿite rulers and, in fact, suppressed Shīʿism to a large extent. They also began the Turkish conquest of Anatolia, which was to result in the establishment of Osmanli and later Ottoman rule. The Seljūqs also supported Ashʿarite theology *(kalām)* against the attacks of the philosophers and sought to strengthen Sunni orthodoxy through the establishment of the traditional university *(madrasah)* system associated so much with the name of their most famous prime minister, Khwājah Niẓām al-Mulk. Although of Turkic stock, they were great patrons of Persian culture. During their rule, Persian prose literature reached its early peak of perfection, and Persian poetry produced some of its greatest masters.

EGYPT AND SYRIA

The destinies of Egypt and Syria, along with the lands in between, such as Palestine, were often intertwined in the Islamic period. As early as the third/ninth century, the ʿAbbāsid governor of Egypt, Ibn Ṭūlūn, who built the magnificent mosque in Cairo that still bears his name, began to assert his independence and extended his authority to Syria. In the fourth/tenth century, the Ismāʿīlī Fāṭimids began their conquest of nearly the whole of North Africa, from al-Ifīqiyyah (present-day Tunisia), and in 358/969 conquered Egypt, claiming the caliphate in the name of their imām. They were the founders of Cairo, which they made their capital. They further extended their rule, over Jerusalem, Mecca, Medina, and Damascus, where they defeated the Ḥamdhānids, and even threatened Baghdad. The Fāṭimid caliphate rivaled the ʿAbbāsids and ushered in a period during which the arts and sciences flourished greatly, especially in Cairo. Threatened by the Seljūqs and later the Crusaders, the Fāṭimids were weakened and finally defeated by Saladin, who also defeated the Crusaders and expelled them from Jerusalem in 583/1187.

Saladin, or Ṣalāḥ al-Dīn al-Ayyūbī, as he is known to Muslims, was a Kurdish general from Aleppo who established the Ayyūbid dynasty, which united Egypt, Palestine, and Syria under Sunni rule, revived the economic life of the region after the long struggle of the Crusades, and set the background for the Mamlūks, originally their slaves, who gained ascendancy and finally established their own powerful dynasty. It was the Mamlūks who finally stopped the onslaught of the Mongols and defeated the Mongol armies in southern Palestine in 658/1260.

NORTH AFRICA AND SPAIN

The ʿAbbāsids did not control the western provinces of the Islamic world, which pursued a separate political history. In Morocco, a descendant of Ḥasan, the grandson of the Prophet, established his own rule among the Berbers with his capital in Fez, which has remained ever since the heart of North African Islam. In Algeria, ʿAbd al-Raḥmān ibn Rustam established another Berber kingdom, called the Rustamid, based on the ʿIbāḍiyyah school, which inherited the perspectives of the Khārijites. As for Tunis, it was ruled by the Aghlābids, who accepted the authority of the caliphate in principle, but who were, for all practical purposes, independent.

In southern Spain and Portugal, or al-Andalus, as the Muslims have known it, the Umayyad prince ʿAbd al-Raḥmān I established the Spanish Umayyad dynasty in 138/756 with its capital in Cordova, which soon became the largest and most cosmopolitan city in Europe. Thus began a rule of two and a half centuries, during which Spain witnessed incredible cultural achievements in nearly every field and the creation of a social climate in which Muslims, Jews, and Christians lived in peace and harmony to a degree rarely seen in human history. Muslim Spain was the locus of not only a flowering of Islamic culture, but also of one of the major flowerings of Jewish culture; the close relationship between the two cultures at the time can be seen in the number of works written by Jewish thinkers, one of the most famous of whom was Maimonides, in Arabic. Spain also became the most important center from which Islamic learning in the sciences, philosophy, and the arts was transmitted to the Christian West and had such a profound effect on later European history. The city of Toledo played a particularly prominent role in this transmission.

In the fifth/eleventh century, Umayyad power waned. Spain became divided into small principalities ruled by local princes (called *mulūk al-ṭawāʾif* in Arabic), making it an easy target for the Berbers of North Africa, especially the religiously fervent and puritanical Almoravids and Almohads, who conquered much of Spain in the fifth/eleventh and sixth/twelfth centuries. But these victories were short-lived. With the power of Muslims considerably weakened, the reconquest by Christians began, marked by the fatal defeat of Muslims in the Battle of Las Navas de Tolosa in 608/1212. Henceforth, Muslims survived only in the mountainous regions of the south, where the Naṣrids ruled and built one of the greatest masterpieces of Islamic art, the Alhambra, in Granada in the seventh/thirteenth century. Formal Muslim rule over the Iberian Peninsula came to an end in 897/1492 with the conquest of Granada by the Christian rulers Isabelle and Ferdinand. After that event, the Muslims who remained were persecuted as Moriscos until they disappeared outwardly from the scene in the eleventh/seventeenth century, although the influence of Islam and its culture persists in Spain to this day.

In North Africa itself, after the assertion of Fāṭimid rule, tribal battles continued between those who paid allegiance to the Fāṭimid caliphate and those who remained faithful to the 'Abbāsids. In the fifth/eleventh century the Sanhaja Berbers, who had spread Islam from Mauritania to the mouth of the Senegal River, united to form the al-Murābiṭūn (which has come to be known as Almoravids in the West), with their capital in Marrakesh, and united much of North Africa and Spain. They were succeeded by al-Muwaḥḥidūn (the Almohads), a dynasty founded by a disciple of the famous Persian theologian and Sufi al-Ghazzālī. This puritanical movement spread as far east as Tripolitania and survived into the seventh/thirteenth century.

With the weakening of the Almohads, local dynasties asserted themselves once again, the Marīnids in Morocco and the Ḥafṣids in Algeria and Tunisia. In the tenth/sixteenth century, North Africa fell into the hands of the Ottomans, except for Morocco, which has been ruled since the tenth/sixteenth century by the *sharīfs,* or descendants of the Prophet, who founded the 'Alawid dynasty. All of the Maghrib, or the western lands of the Arab world, fell into the hands of the French (and to some extent the Spaniards) in the thirteenth/nineteenth century and did not regain independence until the latter part of the twentieth century.

The Mongol Invasion

Although the western lands of Islam were unaffected by the onslaught of the Mongols, the eastern lands were devastated by the descendants of Chingīz Khān, who captured first Central Asia, then Persia, Iraq, Syria, and Palestine, and were only stopped by the Mamlūks in the Sinai Peninsula. The Mongols also put an end to the 'Abbāsid caliphate, thereby bringing about a major change in the political landscape of the Islamic world. With their conquest of Baghdad and killing of the last 'Abbāsid caliph in 656/1258, the Islamic world entered a new phase of its history. After a period of turbulence, several new empires appeared on the scene and dominated much of the Islamic world until the expansion of Western colonialism and the subjugation of most Islamic countries.

The Aftermath of the Mongol Invasion

Turmoil followed in both the economic and political domains in the wake of the Mongol invasion of the eastern lands of Islam. The descendants of Hülagü, who had captured these lands, began to rule, promulgating at the beginning their own Mongolian laws and customs. But soon these rulers, known as the Īl-khānids, embraced Islam, especially when their king, Öljeitü, accepted Islam and became Sultan Muḥammad Khudābandah. It is interesting to note that he embraced Islam in its Twelve-Imām Shīʿite form, and the period from the seventh/thirteenth to the eighth/fourteenth century saw the spread of Shīʿism in Persia, setting the stage for the establishment of Twelve-Imām Shīʿite rule in the Ṣafavid period.

The Īl-khānid period, marked by local powers vying with one another, was terminated toward the end of the eighth/fourteenth century by Tīmūr (Tamerlane), who conquered all of Persia, Iraq, Syria, Anatolia, southern Russia, and Central Asia; his capital was Samarqand, which became a great center of Persian art. Although his vast empire perished with him in 807/1405 when he died on his way to China, his descendants, the Tīmūrids, reigned in Persia and Central Asia into the tenth/sixteenth century, making such cities as Shiraz, Tabriz, and Herat great centers of culture and art, especially the art of the Persian miniature and calligraphy. Moreover, it was one of Tīmūr's descendants, Bābar, who came to India from Afghanistan to establish the Mogul dynasty in the Subcontinent.

Meanwhile, in Egypt, which had repelled the Mongol invasion, the old order continued, and the Mamlūks were able to establish a powerful, stable state, which usually included Palestine and Syria. The state lasted for well over two centuries, from 648/1250 to 923/1517, when it was integrated into the Ottoman Empire. The Mamlūks were Sunni Muslims who emphasized their Sunni affiliation. They were great patrons of the arts, producing some of the finest examples of Islamic architecture, which adorn Cairo to this day, as well as some of the greatest masterpieces of Quranic calligraphy that the Islamic world has ever known. They left their indelible mark on Egypt, and their influence in the arts can still be felt in Cairo.

THE OTTOMANS

The most powerful Islamic state of recent centuries was established in Anatolia by Turkic tribes who had migrated westward from Central Asia through Persia. Although the earlier Turkic dynasty of the Seljūqs was defeated by the Mongols, after a short period Turkish power rose again, around Konya in southern Anatolia and farther west, where various tribes ruled over small municipalities. Soon the "sons of 'Uthmān," or Osmanlis, gained the upper hand, and by 726/1326 they had conquered much of Anatolia, making Bursa their capital. Now known as the Ottomans, they began their conquest of the Balkans in 758/1357, and in 792/1390-91 Bāyezīd Yildirim defeated the other small municipalities and claimed rule over all of Anatolia.

Although defeated by Tamerlane, the Ottomans soon regained their strength and in 857/1453 under Mehmet II conquered Constantinople, which was thereafter known as Istanbul, putting an end to the Byzantine Empire. In 923/1517, Sultan Selīm annexed Syria and Egypt, and the famous Ottoman ruler Sulaymān the Magnificent invaded Hungary in 932/1526 and made the whole of the Balkans part of the Ottoman Empire. The vast empire that spread from Algeria through the rest of North Africa, the Arab Near East, and Anatolia to the Balkans lasted for several centuries, and, despite attack by European powers in the thirteenth/nineteenth century, survived until the end of World War I, when its Arab provinces were divided between the British and the French, its Balkan territories gained independence, and the Turkish heartland became modern Turkey.

The Ottomans claimed to be caliphs who succeeded the Umayyads and the 'Abbāsids, although they were not technically caliphs, but sultans. Nevertheless, they created a political order that functioned in many ways like the other caliphates.

They were staunch defenders of Sunni Islam, while their culture was highly influenced by Persian elements, as seen in both Turkish poetry and painting. They also supported Sufism, which flourished under their rule; some of the orders, such as the Mawlawiyyah and Baktāshiyyah, played an important political as well as spiritual role in the Ottoman world, particularly in Turkey itself. The Ottomans were great builders and created major architectural edifices that can still be seen in Istanbul and elsewhere. They created the last powerful Islamic empire that stood up to the West until the twentieth century and prevented European expansion from following the overland route in its attempt to conquer India and the Far East. The Arab Near East as well as Turkey are heirs to over six centuries of Ottoman rule, as are areas of Muslims in the Balkans including Albania, Bosnia-Herzegovina, Kosovo, and Macedonia.

THE ṢAFAVIDS AND THE LATER PERSIAN DYNASTIES

From the segmentation of political rule in Persia following the Mongol invasion, a powerful religiopolitical movement grew in western Persia under the banner of the Ṣafawī Sufi Order and Twelve-Imām Shīʿism. Supported by Turkic-speaking tribes, the Ṣafavids conquered Tabriz in 905/1499 and soon established their rule over the whole of Persia, which included not only present-day Iran, but also much of Caucasia, the whole of Baluchistan, Afghanistan, and much of Central Asia. They thus established a powerful empire on the eastern flank of the Ottomans and sought to protect themselves from Ottoman domination by appealing to Shīʿism as the state religion (the Ottomans emphasized their support of Sunnism). In a sense the Ṣafavids reestablished the Persian national state after some nine centuries and laid the basis for the modern state of Iran.

They made Isfahan their capital and turned it into one of the most beautiful cities in the Islamic world. Their artistic creations, whether in architecture, tile work, rugs, or miniatures, mark some of the major peaks of Islamic art. Also, despite the migration of many Persian Sunni scholars and thinkers to India, the Ṣafavid period witnessed a major revival of Islamic sciences, especially philosophy. The dynasty, however, which had been originally a Sufi order, turned against Sufism, and conflict arose between Shīʿite *ʿulamāʾ* and the Sufis. Weakened by both internal rivalries and frictions and external pressures, the Ṣafavids were finally defeated by the Afghan invasion of 1135/1722, which put an end to the Ṣafavid dynasty.

For a while Persia was threatened by both the Ottomans and the Russians, who were expanding southward. But in 1142/1729 Nādir, who had been a Ṣafavid general, rose to power and expelled the Afghans and Ottomans from Persia, regaining Georgia, Shirwan, and Armenia in the process. He established himself as king, founded the Afshār dynasty, and became the last Oriental conqueror, capturing Delhi in 1150/1738 and gaining possession of northern India. But his rule terminated when he was murdered by his entourage. After him, the Zands established themselves in southern Persia, while Aḥmad Shah Durrānī declared autonomy in Afghanistan, which finally led to the formal separation of Afghanistan from Persia in the middle of the thirteenth/nineteenth century.

In 1193/1779 the Turkman leader Āqā Muḥammad Khān Qājār seized Tehran and from there the rest of Persia, establishing the Qājār dynasty, which lasted until 1343/1924. Threatened by both the Russians in the north and the British in the south, the Qājārs sought to tread a fine line to preserve Persia's autonomy at least nominally. Much of the territory of Persia was lost, however, at this time to Russia and Britain, but at least the formal and nominal independence of Persia was preserved. However, because of the weakness of the central government, foreign interference and machinations were rampant. Several attempts at reform failed, but the Constitutional Revolution of 1323/1906, which created a constitutional monarchy and the first elected parliament in the Islamic world, did succeed, at least formally, although the struggle for power between the shahs and the religious authorities continued in one way or another until the coming of Reza Shah and the founding of the Pahlavi dynasty. Persia now began a new phase of its life, a period of national assertion combined with modernization. The old struggles, however, between the state and the Shīʿite *'ulamā'* had obviously not disappeared; they took new shape and led finally to the Islamic Revolution of 1979.

THE MOGULS

Islam had begun to spread into the heartland of India in the sixth/twelfth and seventh/thirteenth centuries, mostly through Sufi orders such as the Chishtiyyah. Gradually, local Muslim rule became established, especially during the period known as the Delhi Sultanate, which at times ruled much of northern India. There were also notable small Muslim municipalities in Kashmir and Bengal as well as in the south, especially in the Deccan. In the tenth/sixteenth century, Bābar and his army established their rule over northern India and founded the Mogul (also known as Mughal) Empire, which ruled most of that land from 932/1526 to 1274/1858. The great early emperors, such as Akbar, Humāyūn, Jahāngīr, and Shah Jahān, created one of the most culturally vibrant and wealthy empires in the world.

Dominated to a large extent by the Persian administrative system and the Persian language and art, the Moguls allowed nevertheless a creative interaction between Islam and the local culture of India to take place, which resulted in the creation of some of the finest works of architecture ever built, such as the Taj Mahal in Agra, as well as the flowering of Sufi poetry and music, poetry that was not only in Persian, but also in the local languages. This was also the period that gave birth to Urdu, a language that came into its own in the twelfth/eighteenth and thirteenth/nineteenth centuries as a major vehicle for the expression of Islamic thought and sensibility in northern India and is now one of the major Islamic languages.

After the death of the Mogul emperor Aurangzeb in 1118/1707, the power of the Moguls began to wane as they were confronted with not only external invasions by Nādir Shah Afshār and Aḥmad Shah Durrānī, but also the rise of local Hindu rulers and, most of all, the British, who extended their colonial rule over India and soon annexed the whole of it as part of the British Empire. After the Muslim uprising of 1273/1857, even the nominal rule of the Moguls came to an end, and Muslim as well as Hindu India became a full-fledged colony until the independence and partition of India in 1948.

Islam in Other Areas

BLACK AFRICA

The history of Islam in Black Africa begins at the time of the Prophet, when a number of his companions took refuge in Abyssinia. The eastern coast of Africa became integrated into the Islamic world very rapidly, but Islam remained bound to the coastal areas until the thirteenth/nineteenth century, when communication within the jungle areas, which come close to the sea in that region, made the penetration of Islam into the inner regions of Africa from the east possible. It was from the western region of Africa that Islam spread into the hinterlands, mostly in the savannah that separates the Sahara, inhabited by Berbers and Arabs, from the jungles, which, like the savannah, were inhabited by Black Africans. As early as the fifth/eleventh century, Muslim historians described the Muslim quarters of the capital of Ghana, which was later conquered by the Almoravids, who were then succeeded by local dynasties. By the sixth/twelfth century, most of Ghana had embraced Islam.

There are also records of Muslims in Mali, whose king converted to Islam. Referred to by Arabs as Takrūr, which was in reality only part of Mali, the Muslims of Mali established a major kingdom with a thriving Islamic culture that was in close contact with Muslim centers of North Africa. A city such as Timbuktu became a center of Islamic learning, and to this day the libraries of Mali contain rich collections of Arabic manuscripts. The greatest ruler of Mali was Mansa Mūsā, who lived in the eighth/fourteenth century and who captured Timbuktu as well as the Songhay in the middle of the Niger, which by the ninth/fifteenth century came to eclipse Mali as a Muslim kingdom. The pilgrimage of Mansa Mūsā, accompanied by a vast entourage, to Mecca left a deep impression on the heart of the Islamic world of his day. This kingdom had such famous rulers as Askiya Muḥammad, who, like many eminent Islamic leaders of West Africa, made the pilgrimage to Mecca, where he met the Berber scholar Muḥammad al-Maghīlī, who exercised great influence in that region. Al-Maghīlī preached a form of puritanical Islam, opposed any mixing with local African religious practices, and emphasized the concept of *mujaddid* (which means the renewer of Islam at the beginning of each century)—a concept that has had an important role in Islam in Black Africa to this day, being closely associated with the messianic ideas known as Mahdism.

In the eighth/fourteenth century, the Hausa, who had lived in relative isolation in West Africa until then, gradually became converted to Islam, at first through immigrants from Mandingo who converted the kings of Kano and Katsina to the faith. Later, Fulani *'ulamā'* brought Islamic education to the region and spread the influence of Islam considerably. By the tenth/sixteenth century, Islam was beginning to spread to Bagirmi and Waday, where again the Fulani *'ulamā'* played an important role. At this time also the Moroccan kingdom began to show greater interest in the Saharan salt mines and after several battles established its hegemony over much of this area, especially the land of the Songhay. But it soon lost interest and withdrew, leaving various pashas to rule over local municipalities. For a while the Bambara, who were not influenced to any appreciable degree by Islam, gained power, but at the same time other members of the Mande group who were Muslims began to disperse west and south to the Atlantic, spreading Islam to Upper Guinea and the Ivory Coast.

In the twelfth/eighteenth century, just preceding the European colonization of Africa, a number of major religious movements swept over West Africa, establishing Islamic states based on the appeal of charismatic leaders, some of whom claimed to be the Mahdī. The most famous of these figures was 'Uthmān dan Fadio, born in Gobir in 1167/1754, who soon conquered much of West Africa as both religious leader and ruler. He united many of the fractious tribes and established an order whose religious and political effect persists to this day.

Another of these charismatic figures was al-Ḥājj 'Umar, who lived at the beginning of the thirteenth/nineteenth century. Originally from Futu Toro, he traveled as a young man to Mecca, Medina, and Jerusalem and joined the Tijāniyyah Sufi Order. He returned to Futa Jallon, where his religious and military followers began to increase; he then went to Dinguiray, where in 1268/1852 he declared *jihād*. He fought many battles against both the Bambara and the French and encouraged the emigration of Muslims to avoid living under European colonial rule. He made long spiritual retreats even amid a most active life and was said by his followers to possess extraordinary powers. Killed in battle in 1281/1864, he also left a religious and political heritage that has not been forgotten to this day.

In Arabic the lands lying below the Berber and Arabic regions of North Africa are called *Bilād al-sūdān*, the "land of the Sudan," of which present-day Sudan occupies the eastern region. This latter area, known more technically as Nilotic Sudan, was penetrated by Islam later than western and central Africa. Nubia, which lies north of this region and south of present-day Egypt, was the site of a very ancient civilization that later embraced Christianity and resisted Islamic penetration from Egypt for several centuries. Gradually, however, Arab tribes began to move south, and Nubia became more and more Muslimized until the eighth/fourteenth century, when it became completely Islamic and henceforth was closely historically related to Egypt. The rest of Sudan, except for its southern province, became ever more Arabized, especially from the tenth/sixteenth century onward, when nomadic Arabs pushed into the grasslands of Nilotic Sudan. At the same time a non-Arab tribe, the Funj, pushed north, embracing Islam and completing the Islamization of Nubia and northern Sudan. The Funj were very devoted to Sufism, and during their hegemony Sufi orders exercised great power, a power that continues in many areas to this day.

From the tenth/sixteenth century on the Ottomans also exercised some influence over certain areas of the country now known as the Sudan. The Funj power finally declined in the twelfth/eighteenth century, and in the thirteenth/nineteenth century Egypt sent a mission to subjugate the country that is now known as the Sudan. The Turco-Egyptian domination of the Sudan was to last until the rise of British power in the region in the late thirteenth/nineteenth century. But the situation in the Sudan was such that British colonization was to meet major obstacles in its path. Islamic religious revival was observable everywhere, and in 1298/1881 a charismatic religious figure named Muḥammad Aḥmad proclaimed himself the Mahdī, seeking to unite not only the Sudan, but also the Islamic world in a new religious polity and opposing the Westernization that was beginning to appear among certain classes. He united the tribes and fought against the Egyptian garrisons, which were helped by the British. In 1302/1885 he defeated General Gordon and captured Khartoum, establishing a new Islamic state and a religious organization that is still of great significance in the Sudan.

As for the Horn of Africa, there are records of Muslim establishments along the east coast of Africa by the third/ninth century. Gradually, Muslim kingdoms were created that often paid tribute to the Christian Ethiopian emperors, but such towns as Zaylā' and Mogadishu were already deeply Arabized centuries ago. Although the culture and language were Swahili, there was close contact with the Arab and Persian worlds, and the Somalis, who accepted Islam and spread it in that region, claimed Arab ancestry. In the tenth/sixteenth century both the Ottomans and the Portuguese gained power in the region, the latter burning the city of Zaylā'. Under these circumstances Aḥmad Grāñ, the first of many religious reformers in the area, arose and sought to assert Islamic rule in the region. But Grāñ was finally killed in battle, and Muslim power in the interior began to wane. Along the coast, Islamic Swahili culture thrived as both the Ottomans and 'Umānīs from the Arabian Sea area were gaining greater power. By the thirteenth/nineteenth century, European colonial presence, at first German and British and later Italian, destroyed Islamic rule over the region until the political independence of the area after World War II. But the religious authority of the Muslims on the coast remained strong inland and though their political power had diminished under colonial rule, Islam as a religion began to penetrate to an ever greater degree westward into the heart of Africa, commencing a process that continues to this day. More and more African people became drawn into the Islamic setting represented by the Swahili culture of the coast, in contrast to western and central Africa, where Islam came as a result of the migration of foreign elements, namely, Berbers and Arabs.

SOUTHEAST ASIA

Islam spread into the Malay world beginning as early as the seventh/thirteenth century, but especially from the eighth/fourteenth century through Sufi teachers, pious merchants, and a number of men from the family of the Prophet and ruling classes of the Hadramaut and the Persian Gulf who married members of Malay royal families and brought about conversion to Islam from above. Chinese Muslims also played a role in the Islamization of the Malay world. The role of Sufis, who came from both the Indian Subcontinent and Arabia, was, however, paramount. It was the Sufis who translated classics of Sufi literature from Arabic and Persian into Malay and transformed the Malay language into a major Islamic language. They also began to write original Islamic works in Malay, as can be seen in the writings of such figures as the eleventh/seventeenth-century Ḥamzah Fanṣūrī.

Marco Polo had already detected an Islamic kingdom in Sumatra in Perlak on returning from China to Persia in 691/1292, and Chinese records speak of an Islamic embassy being sent from Samudra to the Chinese emperor in 681/1282. Samudra soon grew into a powerful Muslim kingdom known as Pasai, which lasted until 927/1521, when it was conquered by the Portuguese. Islam gradually spread from northern Sumatra to Malacca, whose ruler, Muḥammad Iskandar Shah, became famous, although earlier Hindu and Buddhist practices continued to prevail for some time elsewhere in the Malay world. By the time of Sultan Muẓaffar Shah, around 855/1450, Malacca's conversion to Islam had become complete. From there, the religion spread throughout the Malay Peninsula from Trengganu to Kedah and Pahang and into eastern Sumatra itself. In 917/1511 Malacca was conquered by the Portuguese, who thus put an end to its Islamic political power, but the spread of the religion continued unabated.

Soon Acheh rose to become the preeminent center of Muslim power. In 930/1524 'Alī Mughayat Shah captured Pasai from the Portuguese and laid the groundwork for the political rise of Acheh. The kingdom of Acheh survived into the eleventh/seventeenth century, reaching its peak with Sultan Iskandar Mūdā, who ruled from 1015/1606 to 1046/1637. After him the kingdom declined and gradually fell apart by the end of the century, but Islam itself became ever more entrenched in Sumatra.

During the tenth/sixteenth century, Arab traders and pious men journeying from Malacca to the Philippines brought Islam to Brunei, the Sulu Archipelago, and Mindanao, where there were Muslim sultanates when the Portuguese and the Spaniards arrived. The Islamic communities that are found in these areas today are remnants of these thriving Islamic kingdoms whose populations have survived despite great persecution and even mass killing of those who refused to accept Christianity by the Spaniards in the Philippines, where the Muslims came to be known as the Moros.

In Java there are records of the presence of Muslims in the ninth/fifteenth century, although many of these Muslims were not indigenous but Chinese Muslims, who left a profound effect on eastern Java. There is also a tomb in Java of a Muslim preacher, probably a Persian merchant and pious man by the name of Malik Ibrāhīm, dated to 822/1419, bearing witness to the presence of Islam at that time. Gradually, the power of the Mahapahit Hindu kingdom waned, and more people began to embrace Islam. This process was accelerated by the arrival of a number of Islamic Sufi preachers from India who played a major role in the spread of Islam into much of Java. As the Muslims gained greater power, they sought to drive the Portuguese from Malacca, but were defeated. They then turned their attention to western Java, which had not yet embraced Islam, and many local battles ensued. Islam penetrated peacefully into the south of central Java through the effort of figures such as Kigede Pandan-Arang, whose lives are interwoven with accounts of miracles and supernatural events and whose tombs are sites of pilgrimage to this day.

The process of Islamization continued in the ninth/fifteenth century eastward to the Moluccas, whose first real Muslim ruler was Zayn al-ʿĀbidīn (891/1486-905/1500). When the Portuguese arrived, they tried hard to replace Islam with Christianity (even Francis Xavier visited the islands), but they were not successful in weakening the hold of Islam in favor of Christianity in that land. Likewise, Islam spread into southern Borneo and the Celebes Islands, where by the eleventh/seventeenth century Makasar had become a center of Islam, resisting for some time the encroaching power of the Dutch.

The eleventh/seventeenth century witnessed the gradual domination by the Dutch of much of what is now known as Indonesia. Even in Java, where the Mataram Empire had succeeded in conquering all the local kingdoms and establishing an empire over nearly the whole of Java, the power of the Dutch and the British grew steadily; battles also continued among various Muslim groups offering different interpretations of Islam. By the thirteenth/nineteenth century the whole of the Malay-speaking world was administratively ruled by the Dutch, the British, and the Spaniards, and small groups of Malay Muslims located in Cambodia and Thailand were being governed by the rulers of those lands.

Islam among the Malay people, who occupy the present-day countries of Indonesia, Malaysia, Brunei, and the southern

Philippines with minorities in other adjacent lands, replaced both the Hindu and Buddhist religions (which began to weaken from the fourth/tenth and fifth/eleventh centuries onward) and local mystical and magical religious practices. Malay became the dominant Islamic language, nourished profusely by Arabic and Persian sources but also drawing from the earlier literary and religious traditions of Hinduism and Buddhism. Although Malay Muslims remained deeply attached to Islam and the center of Islam in Mecca and made pilgrimage (the *ḥajj*) very central to their religious lives, they integrated many aspects of their religious past into their Islamic culture. The shadow play, using themes of the Hindu epics the *Rāmāyaṇa* and the *Mahābhārata*, which has even reached the popular art of Turkey, is an example of this synthesis. In the process of Islamization, which still goes on in the faraway islands, Sufism played a major role from the beginning, and it is to Sufism that one must turn to understand the process whereby Malay was transformed into one of the major languages of the Islamic world.

CHINA

The history of Islam in China is almost as old as Islam itself, for during the Umayyad period Muslims had reached the coast of China by sea as Arabs had done even before the rise of Islam. Gradually, Muslim communities were founded along the coast, while, overland, Persian merchants who traveled over the Silk Route brought not only goods, but also religious ideas with them. There were Islamic communities in many areas of China even during the T'ang period, which ended in the early fourth/tenth century. The Mongol invasion of both Persia and China increased contact between the two worlds, bringing even Islamic astronomy and mathematics to China. Kublai Khān, the conqueror of China, also brought Persians into his military and civil service. Some of these men settled later in Yunnan and formed an Islamic community. Many important figures of state, including ministers, were Muslims.

Gradually Islam spread throughout China, and an indigenous form of Islamic culture with its own distinct artistic and literary forms developed. Many of its features are unique, because it adopted numerous characteristics of the dominant Chinese culture. The degree of participation of Muslims in Chinese life can be seen in the career of the famous admiral of the Ming dynasty Chang Ho, who carried out ambassadorial duties for the Chinese emperor and who compiled a major survey of the Indian Ocean. For the most part, the Ming were lenient toward Muslims, and two of the emperors were even sympathetic to Islam. It was only with the advent of the Ch'ing in the eleventh/seventeenth century that strong opposition to Muslims became state policy and Chinese armies sought to overrun Muslim lands in Central Asia. It is interesting to note that the first Chinese work on Islam by a Chinese Muslim was not written until the eleventh/seventeenth century, when Wang Tai-yü wrote an explanatory work on Islam using Confucian language. His most famous successor, the twelfth/eighteenth-century Wang Liu Chih, continued the approach of seeking to create harmony between Islam and Confucianism; in the same century the Naqshbandi Sufi Ma Minghsin strongly opposed Confucianism as well as the Ch'ing dynasty.

During the thirteenth/nineteenth century, several Muslim uprisings took place throughout China, leading to the death of many Muslims and the complete destruction of a number of Islamic communities in such places as Kansu, Tsinghai, and Yunnan. Later during that century, in 1294/1877, China completed its invasion of Eastern Turkestan, renaming it Sinkiang. Today the Muslim population of this area, mostly of Uighur and Turkoman origin, constitutes the largest concentration of Muslims in China. Also it is in this province that some of the sites of early Islamic civilization, such as Kashghar, continue as thriving communities, despite the persecution of religion during the Communist period.

The Islamic World in Contemporary History

If we were to look at the map of the Islamic world in the thirteenth/nineteenth century, we would see that aside from an ailing Ottoman world, a weak Persia, an unruly Afghanistan, and the heart of the Arabian Peninsula, the rest of the vast Islamic world was colonized in one form or another by various European powers and, in the case of Eastern

Turkestan, the Chinese. The French ruled North Africa, some of western and central Africa, and, after the breakup of the Ottoman Empire after World War I, Syria and Lebanon. The British controlled most of Muslim Africa, Egypt, Muslim India, some of the Malay-speaking world, and, after World War I, Iraq, Palestine, Jordan, Aden, Oman, and the Persian Gulf Emirates. The Dutch ruled Java, Sumatra, and most of the other parts of present-day Indonesia with an iron hand. The Russians gradually extended their dominion over Muslim areas such as Daghestan and Chechnya within what is considered Russia today as well as lower Caucasia and Central Asia. The Spaniards held on to parts of North Africa while they subdued the Muslims of the Philippines and forced many to convert to Catholicism. The Portuguese lost their earlier vast holdings in the Indian Ocean and controlled colonies with only small Muslim populations. It was in this context that late in that century movements for the independence of Islamic countries began, incited both by the religious ethos of Islam and by nationalism, which had begun to penetrate the Islamic world from the West to an ever greater degree, and would become even more powerful during the twentieth century.

With the breakup of the Ottoman Empire at the end of World War I, present-day Turkey became an independent nation and the first and only state in the Islamic world to claim secularism as the basis of its state ideology. Its former European territories, many of which had sought independence earlier, became independent nations, while its Arab provinces to the south, as already mentioned, fell under direct French and

British colonial rule. In the Arabian Peninsula the Saudi family, allied to the aggressive and sometime violent Wahhābī religious movement of Najd since the twelfth/eighteenth century, unified Najd and Hejaz in 1926 and founded the Saudi Kingdom as it is known today. Only the rim of the peninsula from the Arabian Sea to the southern shores of the Persian Gulf remained under the power of the British, who ruled with the help of local shaykhs and princes, or *amīrs.* Egypt retained nominal sovereignty, although in reality it was under the influence of the British.

At the end of World War II, with the wave of anticolonialism sweeping the world, independence movements began throughout the Islamic world. Soon after the war, India was partitioned into Muslim Pakistan, then the biggest Muslim nation, and the predominantly Hindu India, where a sizable Muslim minority continues to live. Pakistan itself was partitioned in 1971 into Pakistan and Bangladesh. Also soon after the War, after bloody battles, Indonesia gained its independence from the Dutch, followed by Malaysia. In Africa, the North African Islamic nations fought against French colonialism, gaining their independence in the 1950s, except for Algeria, where the fiercest battle for independence, resulting in the death of a million Algerians, took place. Algeria finally became fully independent in 1962. Likewise, the Islamic countries of Black Africa gained their independence one after another from the British and the French, although the strong economic influence of the former colonial powers persists to this day.

By the 1970s nearly the whole of the Islamic world was at least nominally free except for the lands that were still contained within the Soviet empire and Eastern Turkestan. With the breakup of the Soviet Union in 1989, however, most Muslim lands of both Caucasia and Central Asia have now become independent. Only Muslim areas captured by the Russians in the thirteenth/nineteenth century and considered part of present-day Russia remain under external political domination, as do the Muslim areas within China and the Philippines along with Kashmir and the Palestinian territories.

The independence of Islamic countries in modern times has not meant, however, their veritable cultural, economic, and social independence. If anything, after political independence many parts of the Islamic world became culturally even more subjugated than before. Moreover, the very form of the nation-state imposed on the Islamic world from the West is alien to the nature of Islamic society and is the cause of great internal tension in many areas. There is, on the one hand, the desire on the part of Muslims for Islamic unity opposed to the segmentation of the *ummah* and the division of the Islamic world not only into ancient and well-defined units and zones, but often ill-conceived and artificial new ones. There is, on the other hand, the strong desire to preserve the identity and character of the Islamic world before the onslaught of modern Western civilization, the invasion of whose values continues unabated. The contemporary history of the Islamic world is characterized by these and other tensions, such as that between tradition and modernism, a tension whose very presence proves that not only Islam but also Islamic civilization is still alive. These tensions, often resulting in upheavals and unrest, indicate that, despite the weakening of this civilization due to both external and internal causes during the past two centuries, the Islamic world is a living reality with its own religious and cultural values, which remain very much alive for the more than 1.2 billion followers of Islam living in lands stretching from the East to the West.

7

Schools of Islamic Thought and Their History

Besides legal thought related to the *Sharīʿah*, already discussed, and the field of the principles of jurisprudence *(uṣūl al-fiqh)*, which is closely related to the Sacred Law, Islamic religious thought has developed in three main channels or disciplines: *kalām*, usually translated "theology"; metaphysics and gnosis *(maʿrifah* or *ʿirfān)*; and philosophy and theosophy *(falsafah, ḥikmah)*. These three disciplines have confronted and interacted with each other in numerous ways during the various epochs of Islamic history.

The Schools of Kalām

The term *kalām* literally means "word," and its use as the name for Islamic scholastic theology is said to have come from the Quran itself, which is the "Word of God" *(kalām Allāh)*.

The founder of *kalām* is traditionally said to have been 'Alī ibn Abī Ṭālib, and its function was to provide rational arguments for the defense of the Islamic faith. Altogether, however, the role of *kalām* is not at all as central to Islam as theology is to Christianity, and many Muslim religious thinkers have been opposed to *kalām*, which is one distinct school of Islamic thought among several others. Not everything that would be called theological in Islam is to be found in the schools of *kalām*, and many Muslim intellectual figures who would be called theologians in English were not known as *mutakallimūn*, that is, scholars of *kalām*.

The earliest Islamic community was caught, like other religious communities, in the throes of disputes over such issues as whether human beings are saved by faith or works, whether there is free will or determinism, and questions concerning the nature of the sacred text as the Word of God. It was not, however, until the second/eighth century that there grew from the teaching circle of Ḥasan al-Baṣrī (d. 110/728), but in opposition to his teachings, the first distinct school of *kalām*, known as the Mu'tazilite school. This school, which dominated the scene for several centuries and produced such famous figures as Abū Isḥāq al-Naẓẓām (d. 231/845) and Abu'l-Hudhayl al-'Allāf (d. 226/840), emphasized the use of reason in evaluating the teachings of religion. It has therefore sometimes been referred to as rationalistic, although this term is correct only if understood in the context of the Islamic universe within which the Mu'tazilites functioned and not in its modern sense.

The Mu'tazilites were known especially for their espousal of five principles: unity *(al-tawḥīd)*; justice *(al-'adl)*; the promise and the threat *(al-wa'd wa'l-wa'īd)*; an in-between position for Muslims who are sinful *(al-manzil bayn al-manzilatayn)*; and exhortation to perform the good and prohibition of doing evil *(al-amr bi'l-ma'rūf wa'l-naḥy 'an al-munkar)*. The first two of these principles concern God, whose Attributes of Oneness and Justice the Mu'tazilites emphasized above all else. The next principle concerns the relation between good and evil actions and the promise of reward and punishment for them in the next world. The fourth principle reflects the Mu'tazilites' way of taking an intermediate position between those who claimed that Muslims who commit a sin are not only condemned to hell but can no longer be members of the Islamic community, and those who asserted that Muslims with faith remain members of the community even if they commit a sin. The last principle, which is emphasized by many other Islamic schools as well, asserts that Muslims must not only follow the teachings of the religion themselves, but also seek to encourage others to perform good acts and prevent them from committing evil.

The Mu'tazilites sought to guard Divine Transcendence in a rational manner, thereby turning God into an abstract unity shorn of His Divine Attributes, whose meaning they refused to discuss for fear of falling into anthropomorphism. Therefore, where the Quran asserts that God is the Hearer and the Seer, the Mu'tazilites claimed that hearing and seeing in this case had nothing to do with what we understand by these Attributes; otherwise we would have an anthropomorphic image of God. Having denied the possibility of our understanding the meaning of the Divine Attributes, the Mu'tazilites then denied the eternity of the Quran, which, being the Word of God, is obviously inseparable from the reality of the Divine Names and Attributes. The Mu'tazilites also applied their rational methods to natural philosophy and developed the characteristic doctrine of atomism, for which Islamic *kalām* is well known. They also developed a "rational ethics" for which they became famous.

Supported by the early 'Abbāsid caliphs, although strongly opposed by many jurists and scholars of *Ḥadīth*, the Mu'tazilites gradually fell out of favor even with the caliphate in the latter part of the third/ninth century. They had practically disappeared from Baghdad by the fifth/eleventh century, although they survived as a notable force for another century or two, as is seen in the monumental Mu'tazilite encyclopedia *al-Mughnī* ("The Self-Sufficient") of the Persian scholar Qāḍī 'Abd al-Jabbār, who lived in the fifth/eleventh century. But this was like the swan song of Mu'tazilism in the heartland of Islam, for Mu'tazilite theology soon became eclipsed as a distinct school of thought except in Yemen, where its tenets were adopted by the Zaydī Shī'ites, who continue to flourish in that land to this day.

It was from this background that there arose the second major school of Sunni *kalām*, called the Ash'arite, named after its founder, Abu'l-Ḥasan al-Ash'arī (d. 330/941), who originally had been a Mu'tazilite. After a dream of the Prophet, however, al-Ash'arī turned against the Mu'tazilite theses and sought to curtail the practice of reason in matters of faith. However, he did not oppose the use of reason completely in religious matters, as had been advocated by Imām Aḥmad ibn Ḥanbal and the Ḥanbalites, who to this day stand opposed to all *kalām*. Al-Ash'arī sought to chart an intermediate course between the extreme positions of groups like the Ḥanbalites and the Mu'tazilites. He insisted on the meaning of the Divine Attributes, but maintained that they were not like human attributes. He asserted that the reality of the Quran was uncreated and eternal, but that its ink and paper, individual letters and words were created. He also emphasized the possibility of Divine forgiveness of human sins and the possibility of the Prophet interceding for sinners in the other world with the permission of God. Altogether he sought to follow a path between transcendence *(tanzīh)* and immanence *(tashbīh)*, and between Divine Justice or Rigor and Divine Mercy.

Al-Ash'arī wrote a number of important works. The most famous as far as *kalām* is concerned are the *Kitāb al-luma'* ("The Book of Light") and *al-Ibānah 'an uṣūl al-diyānah* ("Elucidation Concerning the Principles of Religion"). His thought gained acceptance rapidly, and such students as Abū Bakr al-Bāqillānī made it well known in Baghdad. Soon it gained the support of the caliphate and the Seljūq sultanate and spread over much of the Islamic world. In the fifth/

eleventh century, the later school of Ash'arism, which was more philosophical, arose in Khurasan with Imām al-Ḥaramayn al-Juwaynī, the author of *Kitāb al-irshād* ("The Book of Guidance"), and his student Abū Ḥāmid Muḥammad al-Ghazzālī, the most famous of all Ash'arite theologians and the author of numerous famous works on theology, ethics, and Sufism. Although the author of seminal works on Ash'arite *kalām*, al-Ghazzālī was not, however, Ash'arite in certain of his views and in a number of his later works. In the seventh/thirteenth and eighth/fourteenth centuries the major compendia of Ash'arite *kalām* were composed by such men as Fakhr al-Dīn al-Rāzī, Mīr Sayyid Sharīf al-Jurjānī, 'Aḍud al-Dīn al-Ījī, and Sa'd al-Dīn al-Taftāzānī. The works of these men are taught to this day in Islamic *madrasahs* in the Sunni world along with later recensions and summaries. During the past century, however, an attempt has been made to renovate and reformulate *kalām* by such men as the Egyptian Muḥammad 'Abduh, and certain Mu'tazilite theses and greater emphasis on the use of reason have come to the fore once again.

As for Shī'ite *kalām*, it has always been closer to *falsafah* and emphasizes greater use of reason than what one finds in Sunni *kalām*. Ismā'īlī *kalām* developed earlier than Twelve-Imām Shī'ite *kalām*, and many of the greatest of the early Ismā'īlī thinkers, to whom we shall turn soon, were both theologians and philosophers. Twelve-Imām Shī'ite *kalām* received its first systematic formulation in the hands of Khwājah Naṣīr al-Dīn al-Ṭūsī (d. 672/1273), whose *Kitāb tajrīd al-i'tiqād* ("The Book of the Catharsis of Doctrine") is both the first and the most important systematic work of Shī'ite *kalām*. Many of the greatest later scholars of Shī'ite *kalām*, such as 'Allāmah Jamāl al-Dīn al-Ḥillī, were its commentators. This school of *kalām* continued to flourish into the Ṣafavid and Qājār periods and is still taught in Shī'ite *madrasahs* in Persia, Iraq, Pakistan, India, and elsewhere.

Schools of Metaphysics and Gnosis

A crucial and central dimension of Islamic religious thought, which in fact transcends the formal and external aspects of religion, is metaphysics and gnosis, or what is known in Arabic as *al-ma'rifah* and in Persian as *'irfān*. Metaphysics, as used here, however, means not a branch of philosophy, as it has been understood in modern Western philosophy, but the supreme science *(al-'ilm al-a'lā)* of the Real. Gnosis must not be confused with the sectarian movement known in Christianity as Gnosticism. Rather, it is a knowledge that illuminates and delivers human beings from all bonds of limitation, a knowledge that is accompanied in Islam by the love of God *(al-maḥabbah)* and is based on the foundation of the fear of God *(al-makhāfah)*. This knowledge, which is related to the inner dimension of the Islamic revelation, has its origin in the Quran and the inner teachings of the Prophet and is ultimately none other than the *Ḥaqīqah*, or Truth, alluded to previously. Although in the early centuries of Islam this knowledge was transmitted mostly orally and alluded to in the sayings of the Sufis as well as the Shīʿite Imāms and certain other authorities, it gradually came to be expounded and formulated more openly and systematically. From the seventh/thirteenth century on, it came to constitute a distinct intellectual dimension in the Islamic world.

The first Sufis who wrote doctrinal treatises and began to expound metaphysics and gnosis in a more systematic form were Abū Ḥāmid Muḥammad al-Ghazzālī and ʿAyn al-Quḍāt Hamadānī, both of whom lived in the fifth/eleventh century. In some of his late works, especially the *Mishkāt al-anwār* ("The Niche of Lights"), al-Ghazzālī laid the foundation for later Sufi metaphysical expositions. ʿAyn al-Quḍāt's *Tamhīdāt* ("Dispositions") and *Zubdat al-ḥaqā'iq* ("The Best of Truths") represent important texts of metaphysics and what one might call "mystical philosophy," which set the stage for the appearance of the grand expositor of Islamic gnosis and metaphysics, Muḥyī al-Dīn ibn ʿArabī.

Ibn ʿArabī, who is sometimes referred to as the greatest master *(al-Shaykh al-akbar),* hailed from Murcia, but lived his later life in Damascus, where he died in 638/1240. And it was mostly in the eastern lands of Islam that his influence, as far as doctrinal Sufism is concerned, is seen most strongly over the centuries, though his spiritual influence can be detected throughout the Islamic world from Morocco to Malaysia. The most prolific of all Sufi authors, Ibn ʿArabī composed several hundred works. The most monumental, *al-Futūḥāt al-makkiyyah* ("The Meccan Revelations or Illuminations"), consists of 560 chapters dealing with all the Islamic esoteric sciences and the inner meaning of Islamic rites. But it is his best-known masterpiece, *Fuṣūṣ al-ḥikam* ("Bezels of Wisdom"), that is like the bible of Islamic metaphysics and gnosis. Consisting of 27 chapters, each dedicated to a prophet or aspect of the Universal Logos, the book is considered in Sufi circles to have been inspired by the Prophet of Islam, as claimed by the author himself. Over the centuries, more than 120 commentaries expounding the many levels of its meaning have been written on it.

The outstanding expositor of the doctrinal teachings of Ibn 'Arabī, who in fact left his own imprint on the later interpretations of the master in the East, was his stepson Ṣadr al-Dīn al-Qūnawī, who was the first commentator on the *Fuṣūṣ*. Later authorities in Islamic gnosis—such as Mu'ayyid al-Dīn Jandī, 'Abd al-Razzāq Kāshānī, Dā'ūd Qayṣarī, 'Abd al-Raḥmān Jāmī, Ismā'īl Ḥaqqī, 'Abd al-Salām al-Nabulusī, and others from the seventh/thirteenth to the twelfth/eighteenth century—wrote other well-known commentaries, a tradition that has in fact continued to our own day. Also, Sufi and philosophical figures such as Mullā Ṣadrā and Mullā Muḥsin Fayḍ Kāshānī in eleventh/seventeenth-century Persia, and Shaykh Aḥmad Sirhindī and Shah Walī Allāh of Delhi, who lived in India during the tenth/sixteenth and twelfth/eighteenth centuries, respectively, continued to add to the body of works dealing with Islamic gnosis, even though they were not all simple followers of Ibn 'Arabī; some, like Sirhindī, in fact contested certain theses associated with the Ibn 'Arabian school.

Nevertheless, Ibn 'Arabī is the central figure in the intellectual and doctrinal exposition of Islamic metaphysics and gnosis. Over the centuries, and especially during the second half of Islamic history, this dimension of Islamic religious thought has been of great importance. It has been, in fact, a dominant element in Islamic religious thought in such lands as the Ottoman territories, Persia, Muslim India, and even the Malay world, where the greatest Sufi thinker and writer of that area, Ḥamzah Fanṣūrī, was the inheritor and expositor of Ibn 'Arabian teachings. This dimension of Islamic religious thought, singularly neglected by Western scholarship until recently, is at last receiving the attention it deserves in the West. Furthermore, it remains an important aspect of Islamic intellectual life even today.

Metaphysics is the major field dealt with by this type of Islamic religious thought, but also included are cosmology, eschatology, psychology, and what one might call traditional anthropology. Treatises of the authors mentioned and numerous others deal primarily with the nature of Reality, which they considered to be One. Most of them were followers of the school of the "transcendent unity of being" *(waḥdat al-wujūd)*, which claims that there cannot ultimately be but one Being and one Reality, multiplicity constituting the many "mirrors of nothingness" in which that one Reality is reflected. However, a number of Sufi metaphysicians, such as 'Alā' al-Dawlah Simnānī and Sirhindī, did not accept this formulation and spoke of the "unity of consciousness" *(waḥdat al-shuhūd)* while preserving a clear distinction between the Being of the Creator and the being of the created. The school of gnosis also deals extensively with the cosmos as the theater of theophanies, with the posthumous becoming of human beings, and with the levels of human consciousness and the structure of the psyche in relation to the Spirit. It, moreover, considers man in his cosmic and even metacosmic reality as the universal man *(al-insān al-kāmil)*. This doctrine was formulated in perhaps its most famous version by ʿAbd al-Karīm al-Jīlī, the eighth/fourteenth-century Sufi who was the author of the most famous treatise bearing this title. No wonder, then, that Islamic metaphysics and gnosis reacted on numerous levels with other modes of Islamic thought, such as theology and philosophy, while providing in itself the highest form of knowledge concerning the nature of things and, above all, of that Reality which is the Origin and End of all that exists.

Schools of Islamic Philosophy and Theosophy

Islamic philosophy *(al-falsafah)* was born as a result of the meditation of Islamic thinkers—those who lived in the intellectual universe dominated by the reality of the Quranic revelation—on the philosophical ideas of the Hellenic and Hellenistic worlds and to some extent the philosophical heritage of India and pre-Islamic Persia. Islamic philosophy is not simply the conduit of Greek philosophy for the West, although it performed this function in the fifth/eleventh and sixth/twelfth centuries. Nor is it simply Aristotle in Arabic. Islamic philosophy is essentially "prophetic philosophy," that is, a kind of philosophy based on a worldview in which revelation is a living reality and a source, or rather the supreme source, of knowledge and certitude. It is a philosophy born of the synthesis of Abrahamic monotheism and Greek philosophy, giving rise to a type of philosophical thought that was to wield great influence in both the Jewish and Christian worlds. Although opposed by proponents of *kalām*, Islamic philosophy must be considered a major field of Islamic religious knowledge, and one can no more deny its significance for Islamic thought than one can negate the importance of Maimonides for Jewish thought or St. Thomas Aquinas for Christian thought. In contrast to the view held by so many Western students of Islamic philosophy, this philosophy is part and parcel of the totality of the Islamic intellectual universe, and without it one cannot gain full understanding of that universe.

Activity in Islamic philosophy began in the third/ninth century in Baghdad as more and more Greek and Syriac philosophical texts, especially those belonging to the school of Aristotle and his Neoplatonic commentators, became available in Arabic, transforming Arabic into one of the major philosophical languages and a repository for a great deal of the philosophy and science of Greco-Alexandrian antiquity. The first outstanding Islamic philosopher, Abū Ya'qūb al-Kindī (d. ca. 260/873), sought to create a synthesis between Islamic teachings and Aristotelian and Neoplatonic philosophy, laying the foundation for the *mashshā'ī*, or Islamic Peripatetic school, which is therefore not purely Aristotelian, as the name might indicate.

It remained for the second great figure of this school, Abū Naṣr al-Fārābī (d. 339/950), from Khurasan, to complete the synthesis that al-Kindī was aiming to achieve. Al-Fārābī not only commented on the logical works of Aristotle and Porphyry, but also attempted to unify the political thought of Plato with Islamic political ideas and harmonize the views of Plato and Aristotle (Aristotle, for Muslims, "included" Plotinus, whose *Enneads* was thought to have been written by Aristotle and was referred to as *The Theology of Aristotle*). Many consider al-Fārābī, who was called the Second Teacher after Aristotle, the "First Teacher," to be the founder not only of Islamic political philosophy, but of Islamic philosophy itself.

It was, however, Ibn Sīnā (d. 428/1037), the most influential of all Islamic philosophers within the Islamic world, who brought the *mashshā'ī* school to its peak of maturity and perfection. His magnum opus, the *Kitāb al-shifā'* ("The Book of Healing"), a monumental encyclopedia of both philosophy and the natural and mathematical sciences, exerted vast influence in the Islamic world and even among Jewish and Christian thinkers. There, as well as in shorter works, Ibn Sīnā developed ontology as the foundation of philosophy, for which he has been called by some modern scholars the first "philosopher of being" who left his indelible mark on all medieval philosophy. It was he who first formulated the distinction between necessity and contingency, equating the Necessary Being with God and contingency with all of creation. The themes of the relationship between faith and reason, creation and emanation, spiritual and physical resurrection, rational and revealed knowledge—and numerous other subjects of religious philosophy created by the confrontation between the two worldviews of Semitic monotheism and Greek philosophical speculation—were treated by Ibn Sīnā. He did this in a manner that was to exercise a great influence on many types of Islamic religious thought, including *kalām*, whose proponents, such as al-Ghazzālī and Fakhr al-Dīn al-Rāzī, singled out Ibn Sīnā in their criticism of *mashshā'ī* philosophy.

Toward the end of his life, Ibn Sīnā wrote "The Oriental Philosophy" *(al-ḥikmat al-mashriqiyyah)*, which he considered to be for the "intellectual elite," while the *mashshā'ī* philosophy was for the common public. This "Oriental Philosophy," of whose main texts only fragments survive, is based more on intellection than on ratiocination and views philosophy as a means of transcending the limits of our human condition rather than providing a scheme of things that is rationally satisfying. This dimension of Ibn Sīnā's philosophy was pursued two centuries later by Suhrawardī, the founder of the School of Illumination *(ishrāq)*, and had a profound influence on the later history of Islamic philosophy.

Parallel to the rise of Islamic Peripatetic philosophy was the gradual growth and development of a more "esoteric" school of philosophy associated with Ismā'īlism. The Ismā'īlī school of philosophy was more interested in various schools of pre-Islamic philosophy like Hermeticism and Pythagoreanism and certain strands of older Iranian philosophical and cosmological thought than in Aristotelianism. Starting with the enigmatic and "anonymous" *Umm al-kitāb* ("The Mother Book"), this philosophy grew rapidly in the third/ninth and fourth/tenth centuries and produced such figures as Abū Ḥātam al-Rāzī, Ḥamīd al-Dīn al-Kirmānī, the Brethren of Purity, and Nāṣir-i Khusraw, the fifth/eleventh-century poet and thinker who was perhaps the greatest of the Ismāʿīlī philosophers. The school of Ismāʿīlī thought continued until the Mongol invasion, when it went more or less underground in Persia; it flourished in Yemen and, during the past few centuries, in the Indian Subcontinent.

Ismāʿīlī philosophy, based on the principle of *ta'wīl*, or spiritual hermeneutics, saw authentic philosophy as being identical with the inner teachings of revealed religion, which is transmitted by the imām, and was especially attracted to the esoteric dimensions of the thought of antiquity. It was one of the Islamic schools of thought most receptive to philosophical speculation and, although refuted by Sunni theologians as well as the Twelve-Imām Shīʿites, it played an important intellectual role in early Islamic history, especially during the Fāṭimid period.

Meanwhile, in the eastern lands of Islam, following the domination of the Seljūqs, the attack against *falsafah*, particularly the Peripatetic school, by scholars of *kalām* increased. It was during this period that the celebrated criticisms of *mashshā'ī* philosophy were made by al-Shahrastānī, al-Ghazzālī, and Fakhr al-Dīn al-Rāzī. Among these, the attack of al-Ghazzālī—contained in several of his works, especially his *Tahāfut al-falāsifah* ("The Incoherence of Philosophers")—is the best known, although the critique by al-Rāzī of Ibn

Sīnā's *al-Ishārāt wa'l-tanbīhāt* ("The Book of Directives and Remarks") had greater influence on later Islamic philosophy in Persia and other eastern lands of Islam. Al-Ghazzālī criticized the Peripatetics on several counts, especially what appeared to be their denial of the created nature of the world, God's knowledge of particulars, and bodily resurrection. His powerful pen was able to silence the school of *falsafah* in the eastern lands of Islam for a century and a half, during which time Islamic philosophy flourished in Spain.

The fourth/tenth to the sixth/twelfth centuries mark the golden age of Islamic philosophy in Spain, where the first major figure was the rather enigmatic philosopher Ibn Masarrah (d. 319/931), who was interested in both philosophy and Sufism. The wedding between philosophy and mysticism characterizes many of the later figures of Spain, such as Ibn Ḥazm (d. 454/1063), one of the greatest of Muslim Spanish intellectual figures, both theologian and philosopher; Ibn al-Sīd of Badajoz (d. 521/1127), who was interested in Pythagorean numerical symbolism; Ibn Bājjah (d. 533/1138), the first full-fledged Spanish *mashshā'ī* philosopher, whose *Tadbīr al-mutawaḥḥid* ("Regimen of the Solitary") is outwardly a work of political philosophy and inwardly a treatise on the perfection of the soul; and Ibn Ṭufayl (d. 580/1185), the author of the famous *Ḥayy ibn Yaqẓān* ("Living Son of the Awake")—known extensively in the West as *Philosophus autodidactus*—which deals with the question of the ability of the inner intellect to reach ultimate knowledge.

The most famous and influential Spanish Muslim philosopher, however, was Abu'l-Walīd ibn Rushd (d. 595/1198), known in the West as Averroës, whose influence on Western intellectual life was even greater than that on later Islamic thought. At once chief religious authority in Islamic Law and judge *(qāḍī)* in Cordova and a highly respected physician, Ibn Rushd was also the purest of the Muslim Peripatetics as far as following the doctrines of Aristotle is concerned. He wrote numerous commentaries on the works of the Stagirite and became known in the West as "*the* Commentator"; Dante even refers to him as such in the *Divine Comedy.* Ibn Rushd also wrote on Islamic political philosophy and the question of the relation between faith and reason and sought to answer al-Ghazzālī's criticism of Islamic philosophy in his *Tahāfut al-tahāfut* ("Incoherence of the Incoherence").

Although Ibn Rushd's ideas, interpreted in a way other than the one that comes through in the original Arabic, set the intellectual scene ablaze in western Europe, he did not have a great following in the Islamic world. After Ibn Rushd, with rapid political changes in the western lands of Islam, Islamic philosophy began to wane as a distinct school of thought in that area, becoming merged into the seas of either *kalām* or *ma'rifah,* so that only a handful of notable philosophers, such as the mystical philosopher Ibn Sab'īn and the great philosopher of history Ibn Khaldūn, arose in the Maghrib, or western lands of Islam, during the period following the death of Ibn Rushd. As for the East, philosophy was resurrected by Suhrawardī, Naṣīr al-Dīn al-Ṭūsī, and other figures on the basis of the teachings of Ibn Sīnā rather than the more rationalistic and Aristotelian Ibn Rushd.

During the lifetime of Ibn Rushd, a remarkable intellectual figure named Shihāb al-Dīn Suhrawardī (d. 587/1191) arose in Persia. Although he was put to death at a young age in Aleppo on the charge of heresy (in reality he died because of entanglement in the religio-political struggles of Syria at that time), before his death he founded a new school of philosophy called *al-ishrāq*, or "illumination." Based not only on ratiocination, but also on illumination or intellectual vision, this school sought to integrate the wisdom of ancient Persia and Greece into Islamic gnosis on the basis of the earlier philosophy of Ibn Sīnā, which Suhrawardī considered to be necessary for the training of the mind but not sufficient, since authentic philosophy also requires the purification of the mind and the heart, a prerequisite for the reception of illumination.

Suhrawardī returned philosophy to the status it has always had in oriental civilizations, namely, a wisdom that is intimately related to virtue and the manner in which one lives. His masterpiece, the *Ḥikmat al-ishrāq* ("The Theosophy of the Orient of Light"), is the bible of the school of *ishrāq*, which means both "illumination" and the "light that shines from the Orient," which, in the symbolic geography of Suhrawardī, is not the geographical Orient, but the Orient or Origin of the world of existence itself. Suhrawardī, who wedded philosophy to mystical vision and intellectual intuition, created what came to be known as *al-ḥikmat al-ilāhiyyah* (literally, *theosophia*, or theosophy), which exercised the deepest influence on later Islamic thought in both Persia and the Indian Subcontinent as well as Ottoman Turkey, not to speak of the effect it had on certain schools of Jewish and Christian thought. The school of *ishrāq* remains a living reality to this day wherever Islamic philosophy and theosophy survive and flourish; it has witnessed a revival during the past few decades in the Islamic world and has begun to attract greater attention in the West.

In the seventh/thirteenth century, Naṣīr al-Dīn al-Ṭūsī (d. 672/1273) responded to the attacks of Fakhr al-Dīn al-Rāzī and revived the philosophy of Ibn Sīnā. During the next few centuries the four schools of *mashshāʾī* philosophy, *ishrāqī* theosophy, *kalām*, and Ibn ʿArabian metaphysics, or *maʿrifah*, reacted in various ways with one another, producing many notable figures who sought to synthesize the tenets of some of these schools. It was on the basis of this movement toward synthesis that the School of Isfahan was established by Mīr Dāmād in the tenth/sixteenth century in Persia. A student of the founder, Ṣadr al-Dīn Shīrāzī, also known as Mullā Ṣadrā (d. 1050/1640), brought this school to its peak and created still another intellectual perspective in Islam, called "transcendent theosophy" *(al-ḥikmat al-mutaʿāliyah)*. In his numerous works, especially his monumental *Al-Asfār al-arbaʿah* ("The Four Journeys"), he created a masterly synthesis of the four schools mentioned previously. He emphasized that the three major paths to knowledge open to human beings—namely, revelation, illumination, and ratiocination—lead ultimately to the same goal, and he created a synthesis based on all three. He gave perhaps what became the most satisfying response to the question of the relation between faith and reason in Islamic philosophical thought and produced the most important Quranic commentaries ever written by any Islamic philosopher.

Mullā Ṣadrā became well known in his Persian homeland as well as in Iraq and India. In his own native land his teachings were resurrected in the thirteenth/nineteenth century by such philosophers as Mullā 'Alī Nūrī, Āqā 'Alī Mudarris, and Ḥājjī Mullā Hādī Sabziwārī and are still very much alive in both Persia and Iraq today. As for the Indian Subcontinent, many figures in the twelfth/eighteenth and thirteenth/nineteenth centuries, such as Shah Walī Allāh of Delhi and Mawlānā Maḥmūd Jawnpūrī, were deeply influenced by him. He remains very much a living intellectual figure as Islamic philosophy continues its traditional life in the eastern lands of Islam and finds new life in certain parts of the Arab world, especially Egypt, where Islamic philosophy was revived in the past century by Jamāl al-Dīn Astrābādī, usually known as al-Afghānī, who was a follower of the school of Mullā Ṣadrā before his migration from Persia to the Ottoman world.

In studying the Islamic religion, it is important to remember the long history, diversity of perspectives, and continuous vitality of the various schools of Islamic thought. Far from having died out in what the West calls the Middle Ages, for the most part the life of these schools continues to this day, although a particular school may have died out in a particular region during a certain period. To understand the total reality of Islam as religion and also the interactions of Islam with the modern world, it is necessary to be aware of this rich intellectual tradition of a religious character that is over a millennium old and contains some of the most profound meditations on God, the universe, and humanity in its existential situation in a universe in which human beings are condemned to seek meaning by virtue of being human.

8

Islam in the Contemporary World

Traditional Islam Today

Studies of Islam in the contemporary world usually concentrate on various types of modernism or so-called fundamentalism, whereas the majority of Muslims continue to live in the world of tradition despite all the attacks on the traditional point of view in modern times. To understand Islam today, it is first of all important to realize that the histories of different religions do not all follow the same trajectory. Christianity had the Protestant Reformation in the sixteenth century and *aggiornamento* in the Catholic Church in the 1960s. Judaism has also witnessed the rise of both the Reform and the Conservative schools, at least in the West. Islam, however, has not undergone, nor is it likely to undergo in any appreciable degree, the same kinds of transformation either juridically or theologically. Its religious life and thought remain for the most part within the framework of orthodoxy and tradition. The modernism and so-called fundamentalism that are evident in certain sectors of Islamic society and in certain lands have caused traditional Islamic life to wither, but have been unable to create any significant theological worldview that could challenge the traditional one.

The vast majority of Muslims still practice the traditional rites described earlier, and the rhythm of their lives is punctuated by events related to Islam as traditionally understood. Moreover, the traditional Islamic sciences of Quranic commentary, *Ḥadīth*, jurisprudence, and the like continue as they have done over the centuries despite the devastations brought on the traditional Islamic education system (the *madrasahs*) in many lands. The *'ulamā,'* or religious scholars, continue to wield their authority in the realm of religion and in some lands over political life as well. Likewise, despite being forbidden or circumscribed in certain areas, the Sufi orders prosper in many parts of the Islamic world. During the thirteenth/nineteenth century, when certain elements of Islamic society were emphasizing the importance of modernism, it was primarily the Sufis who opposed modernism avidly. And the events of the past century have only confirmed their appraisal of the nature of the modern world. If anything, Sufism is stronger now than it was at the beginning of the twentieth century, especially among the educated in many lands, such as Egypt. And today it opposes extremism and so-called fundamentalism as it has opposed secularist modernism.

Until a few decades ago, however, the various contemporary strands of traditional Islam—ranging from law to theology, philosophy to art, and literature to Sufism—continued to be expressed in a traditional manner, which became less and less comprehensible to those Muslims who were products of Western educational institutions either within the Islamic world or in the West itself. Western scholarship almost completely neglected contemporary traditional Islamic modes of thought, concentrating its studies on the so-called reformers and modernists. In recent decades, however, the scene has begun to change. Traditional Islam has begun to express itself not only in the contemporary medium of Arabic, Persian, Turkish, and other Islamic languages—to be more accessible to the modern educated classes—but also in European languages, especially English and French, which have become the main languages of intellectual discourse for many Muslims themselves from lands such as Pakistan, Bangladesh, and North Africa, lands that had experienced a long period of colonial rule. Western scholars have also begun to pay greater attention to traditional Islam despite the still prevalent confusion in the West between traditional Islam and what Westerners have come to call "Islamic fundamentalism."

Traditional Islam is like the mountain on whose slopes various geological processes, such as weathering and sedimentation created by streams, take place. It is these processes that can be compared to modernism, "fundamentalism," and the like and that are usually studied by scholars accustomed to the study of change and oblivious to the vast, permanent mountain on whose slopes these changes are taking place. To understand Islam fully in the contemporary world, it is first necessary to comprehend the living nature of traditional Islam, to consider the powerful hold of the worldview of the Quran on the souls and minds of the vast majority of Muslims, and to grasp the truth that the vast majority still believe in the immutability of the Quran as the Word of God, in the reality of the perfect model of the Prophet to be emulated in one's life, in the validity of the *Sharī'ah,* and, for those who follow the path of inwardness, in the efficacy of the permanent and ever renewed teachings of the *Ṭarīqah,* or Sufism.

Moreover, in many domains, ranging from law to the natural sciences and from abstract philosophical and theological thought to art and architecture, there is an attempt throughout the Islamic world to revive and resuscitate the traditional teachings, to live and think more fully Islamically rather than emulate foreign models. This deep yearning also manifests itself on the sociopolitical level and relates traditional Islam in this domain to certain forms of revivalism and so-called fundamentalism, although traditional Islam never condones the use of foreign ideological means to bring about such an end or to reduce religion to ideology. Traditional Islam, while remaining the central religious reality within the Islamic world, is in fact engaged in a battle not only against modernism, but also against those forms of revivalism that employ completely non-Islamic categories of thought and action in the name of Islam and make use of distinctly non-Islamic means to justify what they consider to be Islamic ends.

Millennialism

Although the principle of millennialism is part of traditional Islam, its manifestation in history in its specifically Islamic form as Mahdism has usually stood against traditional institutions. However, later on its effects have been integrated in most cases into the traditional structure of Islamic society. In the early thirteenth/nineteenth century, when, following the Napoleonic invasion of Egypt, the heartland of the Islamic world became fully aware of the dominating power of the West, a number of millennialist movements took place from Muslim West Africa to India. Such famous charismatic leaders as 'Uthmān dan Fadio (who lived somewhat earlier) in West Africa, 'Abd al-Karīm in the Atlas Mountains of North Africa, and the grand Sanūsī in Cyrenaica had a millennialist dimension to their mission, and the Mahdī of the Sudan, mentioned earlier, claimed directly to be the promised Mahdī. Religious movements such as those of Sayyid Muḥammad Bāb and Bahā' Allāh in Persia and Ghulām Aḥmad in what is today Pakistan, movements that broke away from Islamic orthodoxy, and in the case of Bahā'ism from Islam itself, were also of Mahdist origin.

This wave gradually died out in the late thirteenth/nineteenth century, only to rise again during the past few decades following the political independence of Muslim nations without corresponding cultural independence. The very subjugation of Islam, despite outward political independence, which had raised many people's hopes, led to an atmosphere of expectation of Divine intervention in human history. This eschatological atmosphere, which characterizes Islamic millennialism, or Mahdism, was present during the Iranian Revolution of 1979. It was the determining factor in 1979 in the capture of the grand mosque in Mecca by a group of Saudis whose leader claimed to be the Mahdī. It also manifested itself in a strong Mahdist movement in northern Nigeria. Nor has this atmosphere of expectation of eschatological events associated with the coming of the Mahdī disappeared. On the contrary, it is one of the important aspects of the reality of Islam in the contemporary world, as it is of Judaism, Christianity, and Hinduism, not to speak of the primal religions of the North American continent.

Revivalism and "Fundamentalism"

The past few years have also witnessed a great upsurge of Islam on the political plane, which can be seen nearly everywhere in the Islamic world, including in the Iranian Revolution of 1979; the rise of Islamic activism in Lebanon and among the Palestinians; the strengthening of revivalist movements in Egypt and Algeria; the increase of power of Islamic parties in Pakistan, Malaysia, and Indonesia; the rise and later defeat of the Taliban in Afghanistan; and the ever increasing strength of Islamic forces even in the outwardly secular state that is Turkey. Due to a great misunderstanding of these movements in the West, they have usually been grouped together under the name of "fundamentalism," a word originally taken from an American Protestant context and then applied to Islam and other religions.

As far as Islam is concerned, there are many varying types of religious activity, with very different natures, that, unfortunately, are usually clustered together under the category bearing the now vilified name of "fundamentalism." I use the term here reluctantly and only because it has now become so prevalent; otherwise it would be better to avoid such an ambiguous and misleading term completely. There exists in the Islamic world the widely prevalent desire, shared by the great majority of Muslims, to preserve their religious and cultural identity, to reapply the Divine Law that was replaced by European legal codes during the colonial period in many Islamic lands, to draw the various parts of the Islamic world and the Islamic people *(al-ummah)* closer together, and to reassert the intellectual, cultural, and artistic traditions of Islam. These widely held wishes and the impulse to implement them must not be identified purely and simply as "fundamentalism." Rather, most people who share these ideals are traditional Muslims.

Then there is an older puritanical and often rationalistic reform movement, or rather set of movements, that seeks to return to a strict application of the *Sharī'ah* while opposing both Western encroachment and the intellectual, artistic, and mystical traditions of Islam itself in the name of an early puritan Islam considered to have been lost by later generations. To this category belongs the Wahhābī movement, which, in alliance with the Saudi family, finally captured Arabia during the early twentieth century and which remains dominant in that land today. Such movements as the Salafiyyah of Syria and Egypt and the Muḥammadiyyah of Indonesia are related to some extent in their perspectives to Wahhābism and need to be mentioned here although they also differ from Wahhābism in basic ways. One can also include in the category of "fundamentalism" the Ikhwān al-muslimīn, founded in Egypt in the 1920s by Ḥasan al-Bannā', a movement that is still strong in many Islamic countries, especially Egypt and the Sudan, and the Jamā'at-i islāmī of Pakistan, founded by Mawlānā Mawdūdī after the partition of the Indian Subcontinent. The latter continues to be a strong religio-political force to be reckoned with in Pakistan as well as through its offshoots in Bangladesh and among the Muslims of India. All of these movements share in their desire to re-Islamize society and to apply the *Sharī'ah* fully and have usually been peaceful in their methods of achieving this, except in the case of Wahhābism, especially during its earlier history, when it came to power as a result of its political union with the Saudi family in the Najd, and more recently when some who claim a Wahhābī background have been carrying out extremist activities.

Another type of "fundamentalism" of a somewhat different nature, which has come to the fore during the past two or three decades and especially since the Iranian Revolution of 1979, is more activist, revolutionary, and radical than the type associated with Jamāʿat-i islāmī or the Ikhwān al-muslimīn movements. This type of revolutionary movement, with which the very notion of "fundamentalism" is mostly associated in the West today, is seen not only in Iran, where it came to power through the revolution guided by Ayatollah Khomeini, but also among various Islamic groups in Lebanon and among Palestinians, in certain radical circles in Egypt, in the Sudan, in Afghanistan under the Taliban, and in small circles in many other Islamic countries. There are, however, major differences between such movements. For example, the Taliban were inspired by Wahhābism and therefore strongly opposed to Shīʿism and the Islamic Republic of Iran. Although firmly opposed to the West, most of this type of "fundamentalism" often incorporates certain theses of nineteenth- and twentieth-century European political thought, including the very notion of revolution. It politicizes Islam, not in the traditional sense, but in a way that is an innovation in Islamic history. Also, in contrast to the earlier forms of "fundamentalism," which were opposed not only to the imitation of Western culture but also to blind acceptance of Western technology, this more revolutionary "fundamentalism" favors the wholesale adoption of Western science and technology and seeks to gain access to power by whatever means possible, including violence and in some cases even terrorism. Fed by resentment of the situation of Palestine, Kashmir, Chechnya, etc., as well as Western domination over most areas of the Islamic world, which continues in the economic and cultural fields despite the nominal political independence of Islamic countries, this type of "fundamentalism" hopes to provide a solution for the problems of Islamic society by a return to Islamic norms and practices. In doing so, however, it often adopts certain modern theses and value judgments against which it has rebelled. Its power is a reality in the Islamic world, but it is not as great as portrayed in most Western media, where all attempts to retain or return to Islamic principles and teachings are banded together as revolutionary and violent "fundamentalism." Since the tragic events of September 11, 2001, the attempt to identify the whole of the Islamic world with the violent nature of extremism in certain Islamic countries has intensified in the Western media and the reality of the situation has been veiled because of either ignorance or political expediency and therefore the willful dissemination of dis-information. It must never be forgotten that this kind of "fundamentalism" is the other side of the coin of modernism and could not exist without it.

Modernist Tendencies

Nearly every activity in the Islamic world during the past century and a half that has had a modernizing character has also possessed a religious implication. These range from the introduction of Western-inspired nationalism to the adoption of Western technology and the introduction of the Western type of education into various Islamic countries. It is not possible to deal with such subjects here, but their religious implications must not be forgotten. Here, only a few words may be said about modernist tendencies directly related to Islam as a religion.

As early as the thirteenth/nineteenth century, when the impact of European domination began to be felt in the heartland of the Islamic world, there appeared those who believed that the survival of Islam depended on its modernization. In the Ottoman Empire, edicts were passed to modernize the Islamic Law of the land, and similar measures soon took place in Persia as well as in areas under European colonial rule. In such a central land as Egypt, a number of thinkers, such as Muḥammad 'Abduh, sought to modernize Islamic theology through greater introduction of the use of reason, while 'Abduh's teacher, Jamāl al-Dīn Astrābādī (known as al-Afghānī), fought against existing traditional Islamic political institutions in an attempt to unify the Islamic world politically. In India, the project to modernize Islamic education was begun by Sayyid Aḥmad Khān, and in Persia European political ideas finally led to the Constitutional Revolution of 1323/1906 and the establishment of the first parliament in the Islamic world that had the power to pass laws but, at least in principle, with the consent of the religious authorities, or '*ulamā'*.

During the twentieth century the modernist tendencies continued along lines established in the thirteenth/nineteenth century, but with many new developments. In Turkey, Zia Gökalp became the intellectual defender of the secularism proposed by Ataturk when he put an end to the Ottoman caliphate in 1922. In Muslim India, Muḥammad Iqbāl, perhaps the most gifted of the so-called Islamic reformers of the past century, not only proposed the foundation of an Islamic homeland leading to the formation of Pakistan but also espoused the cause of Islamic revival through his moving poetry, written mostly in Persian, but also in Urdu. His prose works, however, reveal much more than his poetry how deeply he was influenced by Western philosophy, especially nineteenth-century German thought.

After World War II, a number of modernists in the Islamic world, particularly in Persia and the Arab world, turned to Marxism. Both Islamic and Arab socialism came into vogue and continued until the downfall of the Soviet Union. Also, a number of Muslim scholars who had studied in the West fell under the sway of Western orientalism and began to criticize traditional Islamic scholarship in the areas of Quranic commentary, the *Ḥadīth*, the *Sharī'ah*, and other basic Islamic disciplines. Movements grew up in such countries as Pakistan to repudiate the authenticity of the *Ḥadīth* and in the Sudan to reinterpret Islam according to only the Meccan period of revelation. A number of Muslim modernists also sought to criticize traditional Islamic thought on the basis of structuralism, existentialism, and other prevalent schools of Western thought, whereas others even attempted to "synthesize" Islam with Marxism.

Although these modern tendencies were once strong and continue to be present despite their relative eclipse during the past few years, they have not had any appreciable impact on Islamic religious thought as such and have not brought about the "protestant" movement within Islam that so many Western scholars had predicted and wished for. The modernist impact on the Islamic world has come much more through the introduction of modern modes of everyday living and thinking, which penetrate the Islamic world through a thousand channels, from modern educational institutions to films.

Modernist tendencies have been confronted during the past few decades not only by so-called fundamentalism, which often seems to have less intellectual substance than the thought processes and works of the modernists, but also by the revival of traditional Islamic thought by those who are as well versed with the modern world as the modernists themselves. Islam in the contemporary world presents, therefore, a picture of a powerful living faith with its still living intellectual and spiritual tradition confronted with challenges of a materially more powerful secular world, which inhabits not only the land outside its borders but also part of its own living space. Various forces are at play in a living Islamic society that is not at all monolithic but that is still dominated, in all of its schools and tendencies, by the message of revelation and religion to a far greater degree than is the case in the contemporary West. Islam today is a living reality faced with multiple problems and challenges, but still deeply anchored in the Islamic tradition and the truths that have guided its destiny since the descent of the Quranic revelation more than fourteen centuries ago. At the heart of this revelation stands the doctrine of the Oneness of God and the necessity for human beings to bear witness to this Oneness in this earthly life. The vast majority of Muslims remain fully aware of this truth today, as they have since the dawn of the religion, and their goal is to struggle to preserve the message revealed to them, to live according to its tenets, and to fulfill the end for which men and women were created despite all the obstacles that a powerful world living in the forgetfulness of God has placed before them today.

Notes

1. In traditional Islamic sources the name of the Prophet of Islam is always followed by the formula "May blessings and peace be upon him" (*ṣalla'Llāhu 'alayhī wa sallam*), while the name of other prophets is followed by "May peace be upon him" (*'alayhi's-salām*). Throughout this book, whenever the word "Prophet" is used in a capitalized form, it is in reference to the Prophet of Islam. Traditional phrases of praise and respect for both God and the Prophet have been omitted.

2. The Quranic translations throughout this book, unless otherwise noted, are based on M. Pickthall (*The Meaning of the Glorious Koran*, New York: New American Library, 1963, and many other editions) and A. J. Arberry (*The Koran Interpreted: A Translation*, New York: Macmillan, 1955 and there are many other editions), with modifications whenever necessary.

3. The date on the left refers to the Islamic lunar calendar, which begins with the migration of the Prophet from Mecca to Medina in 622 C.E., and the date on the right to the Western calendar.

4. The term *imām*, literally "the person who stands before or in front," has many meanings in Islam. In its most ordinary sense, it refers to the person who leads the prayers and by extension the person in a mosque who usually leads the congregational prayers. It also

means one who is outstanding in a field of knowledge and as such it is an honorific title given to certain great Islamic scholars such as Imām Abū Ḥanīfah or Imām al-Ghazzālī. It can also be used as the title of the ruler in classical Sunni political theory, in which case it is equivalent to *khalīfah.* In Twelve-Imām Shī'ism, the term *imām* has been traditionally used in a much more particular sense to refer to the person who carries the "Prophetic Light" *(al-nūr al-muḥammadī)* within himself and, like the Prophet, is inerrant *(ma'ṣūm)*. The number of Imāms (henceforth capitalized in the case of the Shī'ite Imāms) is limited to twelve in Twelve-Imām Shī'ism, of whom the first is 'Alī, the second and third his sons, Ḥasan and Ḥusayn, and the last the hidden Imām, Muḥammad al-Mahdī. For Ismā'īlīs there is a chain of living imāms going back to 'Alī and Fāṭimah, and for Zaydīs, anyone who is able to gain power to protect the Divine Law and rule according to it is accepted as *imām.*

5. M. Lings, *Muhammad: His Life Based on the Earliest Sources* (London: Islamic Texts Society, 1988), 44.

6. Lings, *Muhammad*, 69.

7. These are just some of the more than one hundred most famous names of the Prophet, which correspond to different aspects of his nature, function, and status. "Muḥammad" is derived from the root *ḥamd*, meaning "praise," and means "the praised one." "Aḥmad" is the more inward name of the Prophet related to the same root, whereas "Muṣṭafā" means "the chosen one." The litany of the names of the Prophet plays an important role in Islamic devotion and piety, especially in Sufism.

8. All these quotations are from Allama Sir Abdullah al-Ma'mun al-Suhrawardy, *The Sayings of Muhammad* (New York: Carol Publishing Group, 1990), with certain modifications.

9. Lings, *Muhammad*, 330–31.

10. From Jalāl al-Dīn Rūmī's *Dīwān-i kabīr*, trans. S. H. Nasr.

Recommended Reading

N. Ahmad. *Islam in Global History*, 2 vols. Chicago: Kazi Publications, 2000. A comprehensive survey of Islamic history from its origin to modern times.

A. J. Arberry. *The Koran Interpreted: A Translation*. New York: Macmillan, 1955. An elegant translation of the Quran that captures better than most other English renderings some of the inexhaustible poetic beauty of the original Arabic text.

T. Burckhardt. *Fez: City of Islam*. Cambridge, UK: Islamic Texts Society, 1992. A unique in-depth study of the spiritual, religious, artistic, intellectual, and social life of one of Islam's greatest traditional cities, with numerous insights that apply to the Islamic world as a whole.

——. *An Introduction to Sufism*. Wellingborough: Aquarian Press/Crucible, 1990. A condensed and intellectually precise introduction to the basic tenets of Sufism, written from the Sufi perspective.

V. Danner. *The Islamic Tradition: An Introduction*. New York: Amity House, 1988. An account of both the Islamic religion and the Islamic intellectual tradition from their origin to the present day written from the traditional point of view.

G. Eaton. *Islam and the Destiny of Man*. Albany: State University of New York Press, 1985. A lucid account of the different aspects of Islam by a British Muslim aware of the needs of the Western audience as well as the necessity of presenting the authentic Islamic perspective.

J. Esposito. *Islam: the Straight Path*. New York: Oxford University Press, 1988. A clear account of Islam and its contemporary development by a sympathetic Western scholar of Islam.

M. Lings. *Muhammad: His Life Based on the Earliest Sources*. London: Islamic Texts Society, 1988. A brilliantly written recitation of the life of the Prophet, based on the traditional sources and making available for the first time for English readers an account of the life of the Prophet as seen by Muslims.

S. Murata. *The Tao of Islam*. Albany: State University of New York Press, 1992. The most profound study in English of gender relations in Islam based not only on Islamic sources, but also on certain tenets of Far Eastern thought related to gender complementarity.

S. Murata and W. Chittick. *The Vision of Islam*. New York: Paragon House, 1994. A thorough exposition of various dimensions of Islam, including religious practice, thought, and spirituality based on the *ḥadīth* of Gabriel and the three levels of *islām*, *īmān*, and *iḥsān*.

S. H. Nasr. *The Heart of Islam: Enduring Values for Humanity*. San Francisco: HarperSanFrancisco, 2002. A synthesis of the teachings of Islam, with special emphasis on clarifying misunderstandings currently prevalent in the West about Islam.

——. *Ideals and Realities of Islam*. Chicago: ABC International, 2001. A work written from the perspective of traditional Islam dealing with the Quran, the Prophet, and other basic aspects of the religion, including the relation between Sunnism and Shīʿism.

——. *A Young Muslim's Guide to the Modern World*. Chicago: Kazi Publications, 1993. A summary of the teachings of Islam and various schools of Islamic thought as well as various aspects of Western civilization and the manner in which younger Muslims have to face the challenges of the modern world.

S. H. Nasr, ed. *Islamic Spirituality*. 2 vols. London: Routledge & Kegan Paul, 1987, 1991. A major reference work written by both Muslim scholars and Western scholars sympathetic to the Islamic point of view covering nearly every aspect of Islamic spirituality, both in its foundation and in its historical and geographical unfolding.

S. H. Nasr and O. Leaman, eds. *History of Islamic Philosophy*. London and New York: Routledge, 2001. The most recent and most comprehensive available treatment in English of various schools of Islamic thought, concentrating essentially on philosophy, but including also theology and doctrinal Sufism.

A. M. Schimmel. *Islam: An Introduction*. Albany: State University of New York Press, 1992. A short but in-depth introduction to Islam written with insight and empathy.

F. Schuon. *Understanding Islam*. Bloomington, IN: World Wisdom Books, 1994. The most profound work written by a European on Islam, dealing primarily with the inner dimension of the religion with many references and comparisons to other traditions, including Christianity and Hinduism.

A. S. M. Ḥ. Ṭabāṭabā'ī. *Shi'ite Islam*. Translated and edited by S. H. Nasr. Albany: State University of New York Press, 1992. A clear and authoritative account of Shī'ism by one of the leading Shī'ite scholars of the twentieth century.

Index